GIVE YOURSELF

Grace,

GIRL!

FOR THE FEMALE ENTREPRENEUR READY
TO RELEASE PERFECTION & RECLAIM
YOUR POWER

RASHIDA MCKENZIE

Published in the United States by KH Publishers
www.khpublishers.com

ISBN Paperback   978-1-953237-28-6
ISBN ePUB   978-1-953237-29-3

Printed in the United States of America

Cover and interior design by Dez Carter

First Paperback Edition, March 2022

Dedication

To my husband who loves me like crazy, believes in all of my crazy ideas, and holds it down as I put them in motion.

To my amazing mom who has awakened to her own dreams and desires, and does everything she can to support mine.

To my munchkin and mini business partner, Maya who encourages and inspires me everyday! To my coach

Kellyann who challenged me to write this book and always encourages me to step into my power!

To the village that allowed me to surrender and surrounded me and my husband when we needed you the most!

To the women whose hands will hold my very first book, may you be inspired by it!

Introduction

Introduction

I believe that we live in history's best times to be a woman. Yet, so many of us are still struggling with balance, showcasing our brilliance, and creating businesses that actually provide profit.

The dictionary definition of profit:

Profit
['präfət]

> 1. Noun: A financial gain, especially the difference between the amount earned and the amount spent in buying, operating, or producing something.

Simply put, having more left over than you've spent, which may very well be the case when you look at your finances. However, if you consider how "profitable" you are across other areas of your life, you begin to wonder, is there anything left over for you? If your answer is no, then the truth is, no matter how much money you make, you'll always feel like you're operating in a deficit, and the work-life balance you're seeking will always be in the red.

You have been trying to do things "their" way and, based on what you've been taught to be the "right way." My mission is to provide tools for women like you, to build a business and a life on your own terms.

By the end of this book, I hope you have more clarity and confidence around exactly what it looks like to live life on your terms. You're not in business to prove your worth; you're in business to profit - in every way possible.

Chapter

Oh, Lord Jesus, it's a Fire

"You're not required to set yourself on fire to keep other people warm!

-Penny Reid"

One night, as I lay in bed, I did a quick roll call of my life. Although many of the things on my list brought me happiness, I could not help but feel that something was missing. Roll call went something like this: "Husband? Here! Baby? Here! Business? Here!" As I kept going down the list, I got to joy. "Joy?" Silence. "Joy?" The silence thickened. "Has anyone seen Joy?" Still, no answer. So, I moved on. Next up, "Peace?" Again, silence. "Is Peace here?" Nothing. I was certain they were both present at one point, but my peace and joy must have held hands and made a run for it because they could no longer be found.

I was finally doing something I dreamt about; owning my own business. I had built a first-of-its-kind concierge service for executive & entrepreneurial moms in the Washington D.C. area. My company specialized in ensuring that their life ran smoothly, and they had time for the things that mattered the most when mine was secretly and slowly falling apart.

My attendance to my family, business, and most of all, myself was rapidly declining, and I didn't understand why. Suddenly, I had lost the spring in my step. I couldn't get out of bed a second earlier than I had to, although I needed every second I could get just to maintain it all. Every night, I would rhetorically ask my husband what time he needed to wake up for work, weaving in intentions to appear collaborative in my efforts to be a willing participant in managing our life.

I knew *exactly* what time he had to be up. I wanted him to remain convinced that I was eager about getting up before him, getting a jumpstart, and even squeezing in a workout session all before he left for the day. But when the alarm clock crowed, I could not move. He'd shake my shoulder to wake, but I would not budge. Unfulfillment anchored with dissatisfaction had weighed me down. "Tomorrow," I declared, implying that it would be a better day, and I'd be energized to get myself up. However, tomorrow never came. He'd give his best effort to get me up, and I'd just bury myself deeper into the blanket and turn over. We played this game for months until he got tired of riding the merry-go-round with me.

"Wake me up tomorrow," I said routinely, one evening.

"Yeah, ok," he responded sarcastically.

The moment came to a screeching halt. My husband was clearly frustrated. However, as much as I loved him, his frustration didn't move me. There wasn't anyone more frustrated than I was. Well, perhaps the preschool director at my daughter's school. She was also growing increasingly frustrated. She noticed my escalating tardiness and, one day, politely pulled me aside to tell me how much more "beneficial it would be" if I "could start getting my daughter there before circle time."

"I know!" I wanted to scream. I wanted to get up and get her there on time, but every tactic that I tried failed to motivate me to move any faster. I took my husband's sarcasm as a challenge to encourage me to make a change. He understood that one of the quickest ways to motivate me was to tell me or imply that I couldn't do anything. However, this time was different. I didn't meet the challenge with the zeal I once did. In fact, the next morning rolled around, and I still could not manage to pull myself together. There was something *really* wrong. This time, I just could not force my way, work harder, or want it badly enough—nothing I did made a difference.

Perhaps you, too, have strategized, simplified, streamlined, sacrificed, and stretched, yet you still feel stuck. You know that feeling when not even 10-hours of sleep in the most comfortable bed would solve the level of tiredness you feel in your body? If you are here, it means you've hit a slump. That's what we call it in sports - when you're no longer able to perform the way you used to. You're used to dominating, doing what you've got to do, and getting it done.

You're in a slump when:

- You're bored in your business or career and find yourself daydreaming about being at home or anywhere else.

- You dread going home because you're overwhelmed by the second shift as soon as you walk in the door.

- You can't remember the last time you did something just for fun or to relax. Even self-care has become another chore on your checklist.

- You can't quite put your finger on what's wrong, but you just don't feel good.

- You seem to injure yourself or get sick far more often than typical for you.

- You are usually driven and productive, yet you are inexplicably unmotivated and un-enthused.

Perhaps you see yourself in a few of these or even all of them. I've found that a slump typically boils down to one telltale question, "How did I get here?"

If you've ever asked yourself this question, then girl, you're deep in it. The good news is, that's precisely the question that you should be asking, so you know you're aware and ready to pull yourself out.

We'll undoubtedly get to the bottom of that question in this book, but before we do, let's pause here for a second. Let's agree that you won't breeze past questions as they come up. You know how we do; we push through, ignoring all of the smoke signals warning us of imminent danger. I learned this lesson the hard way, but as Oprah Winfrey says about missing the signs, "First God throws a pebble, then he'll throw a brick."

Full Blown Burnout

While my business was still in its infancy, I had also taken a part-time job working overnights at a hotel. I worked at the hotel, from 11 PM - 7 AM. While on my overnight shift, I took advantage of my time and worked on marketing and communication for my business. I dialed in on my email campaign to potential clients. I was focused, and new clients started to roll in. Sounds great, right? Well, not so much. I hadn't thoroughly thought through who would be responsible for executing the promised services. So, I ended up as a decision-maker and service provider in my business, a.k.a, doing everything. This resulted in me having to balance my time between work, business, and family. Now, don't get me wrong, financially, things were looking good. However, I was constantly irked by that inexplicable feeling of unhappiness and unfulfillment but didn't dare say it aloud because I didn't want to seem ungrateful.

After a typical evening of work at the hotel, I was on my way to a client. As I drove along the street, belting Anita Baker's "Angel" at the top of my lungs, I danced with the steering wheel in my hands. This was one of the many tactics I used to stay awake during my commutes, along with a newfound caffeine addiction. This particular morning would prove to be anything but typical. I sat at an intersection, waiting to make a left turn. An approaching car drove along in the opposite direction on this bi-directional road. It appeared that they weren't going to cross into the intersection but would turn off the road. However, the car continued straight along the road as I chose to make my turn, and boom, I smashed my car right into the driver's side door. Stunned! I sat there in disbelief.

I was just a block away from my client's house when this all took place. As I sat in my car, with my bumper hanging off, in the middle of the intersection, instinctively, I bypassed calling my insurance company or my husband, but instead,

I picked up the phone and called my client. My client! Crazy, I know, but I kept thinking about how not showing up for my meeting would ruin my reputation. I hung up the phone, laid my head on the steering wheel, and cried. Ironically, I wasn't crying because I was in an accident or hurt. I cried because the accident threw a wrench in my plans. So, I went and got myself a rental car and was back in business the next day! So, I thought.

My disregard for that accident was the tipping point. Before I could bat an eye, my slump had turned into full-blown burnout. The smoke had become a full-on fire, and that's why I couldn't get out of bed. My life was talking to me, but I wasn't listening. I didn't have time to listen, not when I had a business to run, a baby to raise, and a husband to keep happy. The signs had been simmering for a while.

1. Not Getting Enough Rest

I would come home and wait for my mom to arrive around 8 am, hand off the baby, crash no later than 10:30 am, and then head out of the door. That is two, maybe three hours of sleep, maximum. My constant need for caffeine and relentless cravings for junk food I easily accommodated in the hotel snack bar was a tell-tale sign of my fatigue. Plus, I always seemed to have a bad attitude and was easily irritable. When you physically over-work yourself and do not allow your body and mind a fair chance to relax and recover, this is the first step to embarking down the road to burn out, which is dangerous. Believe me. I know how so many of us struggle with the idea of resting. We tied our worth directly to our work. But just know that you learning to relax is revolutionary!

2. Tying Your Self-Worth To Your Performance

One of the first questions that we generally ask someone when meeting them is, "What do you do?" So many of us have come to define ourselves based on our occupations. You become your career, tying your identity and self-worth to your success. I called my client after the accident, not to inform them about it, but because I was worried about my reputation. Although any adverse impact would reflect on my business, I took things personally and was concerned about tarnishing my name. There's a term for this, and it's called enmeshment. This is when the boundaries between your work and personal life become blurred, and you allow your job or business to eat into every area of your life. I couldn't even have a conversation without bringing up my business.

When a business becomes the most significant thing in your life, at the expense of your sanity and your family, that's when it can become a problem. When you tie your self-worth to your ability to perform, the success and failure you experience will directly affect it. When you put your ego on the line like this, you not only set yourself up for disaster, but you'll blow past burnout into breakdown.

Ain't nobody got time for that!

3. Putting Too Much Pressure On Yourself

In a culture where we're constantly comparing ourselves to what other people are doing, how they seem to be progressing, or what they're doing with their lives and businesses, we cause ourselves undue stress and sadness. If the comparison is the thief of joy, then pressure is the enemy of progress.

You're probably a first-generation business owner, and you may have even been the first in your family to go to college. Still, the level of expectation you carry for yourself is as if you inherited the business with detailed instructions. I earned enough in my business and had replaced my salary, and even that didn't feel good enough, especially with all the Facebook ads touting people who were claiming to earn six figures in six months. Instead of focusing on your own evolution, you can get caught up in trying to get ahead, do it better, faster, and even more amazing than others that you're not present, or even enjoy the progress you've made!

4. Exchanging Money for your Mission

This is the part that most of us miss in our hurried lives: our mission. I believe you know *exactly* what it is that you want to do. Call it an inkling, a knowing, calling, or your purpose. We all have it. And I genuinely believe that you already know what it is, or you wouldn't be reading this. Don't ignore it anymore. Don't allow your hurriedness to make it hard to hear amid all your distractions. Don't become disconnected and discouraged because you're not doing what you love to do. Find a way to incorporate the things you love into your life now. No matter where you are in life, it's truly never too late to answer your calling.

- Did you know that Vera Wang didn't begin designing clothes professionally until she was 39 years old? Before that, she was a fashion journalist. After designing her own wedding dress, she opened a bridal boutique and soon launched her signature collection.

- Martha Stewart was nearly 50 years old before she signed her deal to develop the *Martha Stewart Living magazine.* But she was always crafty. Martha, too made her own wedding dress. After renovating her first home, she decided to open a catering company from her kitchen. She made everything from scratch, and the recipes

she used eventually became the basis for
her famous cookbooks.

You can start utilizing your gifts and talents right
now. If you've found that you no longer enjoy what
you're doing, I would be willing to bet that you've
built a business that's left out the things you actually
like to do. We take jobs, start businesses, accept
titles we have zero passion for and wonder why
we're miserable. Getting paid isn't a prerequisite
to doing the things that bring you joy. Girl, get a
hobby. Doing what you love creates a meaningful
life, but you don't leave time for what lights you up
when you let the little things pile up. Consequently,
we limit ourselves to taking one of two paths, both
of which can cost you if you're not careful.

Path#1: Give up

During a slump, you will undoubtedly question
whether or not what you want to do is actually
meant for you. Call it opting out, giving up, or

throwing in the towel, so many women contemplate closing their business and giving up on their goals because the thought of adding anything else to their plate feels like too much. So, what we convince ourselves we're selecting peace instead of doing what truly matters to us. This is where you have to be honest with yourself. Only you know the truth. But I believe that we tend to press pause as a way to stall, delay, or procrastinate. So, you don't really find peace because that initial spark never fades. You always feel it. We'll touch more on that in a minute.

It's easy to attribute your frustration to the many demands you have on you. However, until you get to the root of why you're in a slump, you'll keep hopping from place to place and passion to passion, hoping that something sticks. You will find yourself searching to find the harmony that's been eluding you.

Path #2: Go harder

Now, some of you go to the other extreme when it feels like something isn't working for you. You become more determined to prove you can do it, and you head in the opposite direction of giving up; you go harder. You work longer hours, terrorize yourself over the tiniest of details, and double and triple-check everything before letting it out of your sight. You get busier in your business. But afterwhile, you realize that doesn't work well either. It's actually unproductive. You keep mulling over the minutia so you can feel like you're working, but you're not really moving. You're living your life on the treadmill. You'll likely end up mentally and physically exhausted at the exit anyway.

You've gotten to know me a little bit by now. Can you guess which path I took? If you guessed path #2, then you got it. I dug my heels into my business even more profoundly. I began hiring people to help manage and optimize my company. I signed up for more activities with my daughter and wracked my mind for creative date night ideas. I was determined to continue to deliver the level of service everyone around me was accustomed to, even if it depleted me. They depended on me.

Are you more of a path one or path two kind of girl? Either way, your problem will not be solved by hiring more people, signing up for another "Mommy & Me" class, or a candlelight dinner at Ruth Chris. Those are actually the benefits you experience when you break out of your slump. Your problem is not even your business or anything you aspire to do. It's what you believe about yourself, what you can have, and the way you think you have to go about getting what you want. I'm also willing to bet that you haven't been clear on exactly what you want, and that's why you don't know how you got here. You never chose to be; it just, sort of, happened. I know that may be hard to digest but, the good news is that it's entirely within your power to change if you choose to. When you understand where this comes from, walking away will no longer be an option—because you know it is entirely within your power to change it.

The world needs what you have to offer, but you cannot operate at your best when you are burnt out. So, although it doesn't feel like a good place to be, your slump has presented you with an opportunity. You are now at a crossroad where you get to intentionally choose to do it differently and position yourself to lead with longevity and lasting impact. While others are pushing you to "hustle harder," I'm going to teach you another method of creating happiness, fulfillment, and flow along with financial success. The solution you're seeking is smack dab in the middle of the two paths discussed earlier. It isn't to go harder or give up, but to give yourself grace, girl! There's nothing you have to do to deserve your success, it's already yours, but you've got to own it. Overloading yourself non-stop, as if you need to get everything done at once, will not get you to your goals any faster.

Now, let's look at how you got here in the first place so you can move forward without apology and take your time, talent, and energy back!

Chapter

What Got You Here Won't Get You There!

"It's not like before
I have children, to take care

"It's not like before when
I could rehearse 15 hours
straight—I have children,
I have a husband. I have
to take care of my body.
I just feel like I'm just
a new woman in a new
chapter of my life, and
I'm not even trying to be
who I was.

-Beyoncé

I just feel like a new woman
with the majority

*T*hink back to the starting line in your life; the time frame when you took the reins of responsibility. You probably felt pretty invincible, huh? You had this insatiable drive to show the world what you were capable of. You walked into a room, and your body language practically yelled, I've arrived! Eager to prove yourself, you did whatever it took. You were the first to arrive and the last one to leave. You did everything you were told in hopes of rising to the top.

The minute I turned the tassel on my college

graduation cap, I hit the ground running *hard*.

A few months before my college graduation, my professor tipped me off about a new apprenticeship program that CBS was launching to increase diversity in their newsrooms. It was highly competitive, and there would only be one spot in each of the few selected markets, but none in my hometown of Minnesota. So, I scraped my money together and bought a plane ticket to Pittsburgh, PA, to pitch myself for the program. By the time I finished my pitch, I knew the job was mine. However, there was a catch. I flew over 700-miles for a job that only paid $10 per hour. I instantly realized that getting my own place was now out of the question.

Nonetheless, I accepted the position without any hesitation. I understood the opportunity this presented for my career. It was the sliver in the door I needed, and I planned to take it and break that bad boy down.

I put out a call to find anyone who would let me sleep on their couch for the next few months. Eventually, I found a family member, of a friend of the family, who had a spare room. I would be living with a complete stranger. But I didn't care. It was a tiny sacrifice for a big dream. So, I crammed my stuff into my Mazda and drove off into the sunset. I was on my way.

By the time the sun rose each morning, I was already at the station. It turns out I barely used that spare bedroom because the TV station had become my second home. I was focused on making the most of this opportunity. I hustled. I nestled under the wing of Casey, the best producer on set, and she taught me everything she knew. I volunteered for all the jobs no one else wanted and worked in every department. Then one day, a producer called in sick. The station was short-staffed, and they needed to fill this role. This was show business, and as the saying goes, "the show must go on." Biting the specs of skin on his bottom lip, the news director pondered out loud who could fill in and produce the show. "She can!" Casey's finger darted at me in the back of the room, the area reserved for the interns.

She began to spill out all of the work I'd been doing with her. It felt as if an overhead spotlight was panned on me. So, I met its focus and sat up straight in my chair. This was the moment I worked so hard and trained for. I was ready, and I killed it! I filled in as the producer and executed flawlessly. This was the chance I needed, and the payoff was securing a full-time role with the station.

The new role also resulted in higher pay, which afforded me the luxury of getting my own place. I was beginning to find my way, and I started plotting my next course; to get on-air. One sure-fire way of getting to that next level was to ride along with reporters, so I jumped at every chance I could get! Once their segment wrapped, they would let me gather footage for my video reel, giving me the opportunity to produce my own content and add to my tape. I had my eye on the prize, and nothing would stop me from achieving my goal.

Before I knew it, I had been swept up in the tornado of the TV news world. I adopted the weird and stuffy speech pattern that newscasters are known for. I quickly progressed through the ranks and loved post-college life. It was fast-paced and competitive, which ensured I was never bored. But the luster didn't last long. After just about two years of office politics and lack of creative control, the haze began to lift, and it wasn't long before it became evident that staying competitive and achieving success meant constantly conforming.

"If you're going to make it in this business, you're going to have to take those ropes out of your head," one of the few black faces in the newsroom told me, referring to my braids. Taking his advice to heart, I found a beauty shop that pressed my hair so straight so often that it fell out. I also lost weight to compensate for the 10 lbs. the camera supposedly adds. It may seem extreme, but we've all been guilty of compromising ourselves to reach our goals, especially if you've worked in Corporate America.

You don't always realize it because it feels more like enthusiasm than compromise when you're young, but when is the last time you've even come close to that type of eagerness for yourself as you have with your employers.

- Showing up even when you don't feel like it—because you know that is what's necessary for company growth.

- Getting dressed and putting your best foot forward because it makes you feel good—even if there's no one around to see your work.

- Taking the time to prepare for meetings— because you wouldn't wing it at work.

You don't have to replicate the corporate model or hustle culture and call that success. I know that's what you're used to, but you're here because you're being called to create your own.

Instead of losing more weight, I began to weigh my options. Was I really supposed to work 60+ hours per week for the rest of my life doing something where I had to give up so much of myself? I started doing a poll in the newsroom, posing a simple question to veterans who were "Ahh-mazing" at their job. "Is this the life you pictured?" The overwhelming response was, "No."

I recall one of the answers very clearly. Connie, an executive producer on the prime-time show, sighed heavily and said, "You know it's not. But I have children now who depend on me for life and dental insurance, so there's no going back now," she laughed.

I didn't find what she said funny. Don't get me wrong. I'm a hard worker, and I have a strict work ethic, but I just couldn't help but feel that this wasn't going to work for me.

Thomas Merton says, "Some people may spend their whole lives climbing the ladder of success only to find, once they reach the top, that the ladder is leaning against the wrong wall." When you come to the realization that you're leaning against the wrong wall getting off of it is giving yourself grace. Sometimes the things you think you want and are working towards are no longer what you really want.

So. how do you know the difference between when

you're giving up and getting off the wall? When you give up, you know there is more that you can do—but don't. It is usually an emotional decision versus a well-thought-out decision to do something else. I acknowledged that my time was up and began searching for my next golden opportunity. The station was aware of my pursuit and repeatedly offered me proposals to stay. My mind was made up. Elevation was in sight when the doors opened for a chance to do Public Relations for a minor league basketball team back in my hometown. Excitement set in, and I packed my bags and found myself headed back home.

The rug was swept from beneath my feet almost immediately. Within one month of being on the job, the team went belly up. Here I was, back home with my parents and jobless. I began questioning myself. This was my first *real*, grown-up decision, and it landed me on my behind. This was not the life I envisioned when I took off at the starting line. After spending a few weeks curled up in my childhood bed, I was finally able to land a new job, but it was just that, a job, nothing that I wanted to do long-term.

The real problem was that I wasn't navigating the world with my own map. My decisions weren't based on my passion or what I deeply wanted in life, but instead based on what I thought would bring the most approval and, more importantly, get me paid.

Most of us don't know what true and authentic success looks like until we dig deep enough to identify it. Initially, you set out for the most popular and widely known destination. And if you are wise enough to be a bit more targeted, you then supplement a broad perspective with a more focused path, yet still the most profitable. Either way, what's driving us isn't our innate passion, purpose, or gifts. We are driven by a force of decision-making that has been inherited and influenced throughout our lives. One that often prioritizes financial success over peace of mind and perception over reality—often celebrating the appearance of success over actual success. But what if I told you that there is another way that doesn't require working "fifty-leven" hours, pulling all-nighters, and missing life's most precious moments? You can still get you paid, but you're going to have to prioritize differently. Or you can stay exactly where you are, continuing to play it safe, keep your head down and make a great living, but ask yourself would it be a great life?

The good news is that just like you created this mode of operation, you can create something else, only this time what you really want. You're the boss! So, if you've built a business model and environment where the expectation is to constantly burn the candle at both ends, being away from your family and skipping vacations—that ends here.

There are seasons in your life that require you to shift, and to be able to change as the seasons in your life do is what allows you to grow – to give from a place of overflow versus overwhelm.

You have to intentionally decide to cultivate a business that aligns with your life and, ultimately, your core values. Still, you must first understand what your core values are. Your core values shape your beliefs, which dictate your behavior and guide you to make decisions. They help you make decisions that will play into your strengths, wants, and needs. If one of your core values is family, but you are so heavily scheduled doing other things that you don't have time to spend with them, then your business will conflict with your life.

If another core value is dependability, but you don't have a system to respond to people in a timely manner, then you'll feel like you're failing when correspondence slips through the cracks. Perhaps compassion is one of your core values; however, the people who work for you never see you care for yourself. As the leader, that sends a message about how comfortable they can feel about asking you for time off.

Your business values flow from your personal values, so you've got to be clear on what they are. People can't respect principals they don't know about. You won't prioritize principals you don't really care about. Your values must align with your vision, and your business is just a vehicle to achieve your personal goals in life. So, when you're clear on core values, you can formulate your definition of success and don't have to compromise.

It may take a while to feel that initial confidence you felt when you first started climbing the ladder, but that's because you've always complied with system norms. Now, you possess enough life experience to know better. If you have created something that doesn't work for you, then accept that it doesn't work. When you know better, your spirit, that internal compass you have inside, won't allow you to go back! There is absolutely nothing wrong with you for no longer wanting to operate the way you once did. Unlike when you decide to take off at your original starting line, it's not about intensity but instead intentionality.

Space for Grace

Your approach to the way you work likely looks a lot different than it did when you were younger. Most likely because the values that resonated with you then were a lot different. In order to make sure that you're being intentional about it moving forward, you have to align your future vision with your core values now. You're going to have to acknowledge your inner "Golden Girl!" I call mine

Agnes, and she is the 80-year-old version of me.

When her grandchildren and great-grandchildren gather at her feet, what values will her life have modeled as important to her? What advice will she give them based on the life that she has lived? That's not something you decide when you're 80 years old. You give grace to your future self by deliberately deciding who you're going to become today. When we're young, we tend to overlook her presence. We don't heed her wisdom or consider the toll our choices, fear, and hesitancy have on her. Depending on how close you are to your golden girl, you can actively feel her presence. You see her in that sprout of gray, and you feel her in the crackling of your knees when you walk up a flight of steps.

What values nurture her vision? Acknowledging your golden girl makes sure that you don't just commit to the outcome (or your income while ignoring who you have to become in order to get there).

First, highlight all the core values you want your golden girl to exemplify on the chart below. Here is a list of 50 values to get you started. Feel free to add to the list.

Next, circle 3-5 values that really resonate with you.

Adventure	Affection	Beauty
Career	Caring	Change
Clarity	Commonality	Communication
Connection	Contributing	Cooperation
Creativity	Encouragement	Excellence
Faith	Fame	Family
Forgiveness	Freedom	Friendship
Generosity	Goodness	Grace
Honesty	Innovation	Integrity
Intelligence	Involvement	Joy/Play
Kindness	Learning	Love
Loyalty	Openness	Opportunity

Physical Well-being	Pleasure	Power
Pride in Your Work	Quality	Relationship
Respect	Security	Speed
Strength	Success	Teamwork
Wealth	Wisdom	

Now, let's break down what each value means to you. It's all about how you view it. Here is an example of what "health" means to me:

- **Health** = I am taking care of my body and mind through exercise, eating right, practicing self-care, and setting firm boundaries.

1. _____ = _____

_____

2. _____ = _____

_____

3. _____ = _____

_____

4. _____ = _____

_____

5. _____ = _____

_____

CHAPTER

Unboxable

"When you're living for the approval of strangers and that is where you derive all of your joy and fulfillment, one bad thing can cause everything to crumble."

-Taylor Swift

*W*hen you're a woman who is used to excelling at most things in your life, excellence becomes the expectation. It's not only how you expect yourself to operate but also how everyone else around you should operate. I'm willing to bet that the reason that you're so good at many of the things that you do is that you've been doing them for such a long time.

In elementary school, you got good grades, tried out sports in middle school, made the team, and became the captain. Once upon a time, you had the "Midas touch." Everything you set out to do pretty much turned to gold! At a very young age, you also learn that if you do things "the right way," according to someone else's standards of what's right, then you will be applauded, celebrated, and even rewarded. We become enslaved to needing the validation of others, and we constantly look to others for acceptance and acknowledgment. This is why so many women struggle with confidence. So, it's no surprise that when it's time for us to do something which may not warrant the validation we have grown used to, we hesitate to go for it—we're afraid of deviating from the formula.

In her book, *Lean In*, Sheryl Sandberg shared how "a woman won't confidently pursue a new position unless she feels like she is 100% ready compared to a man who will apply when he feels like he is at least 60% qualified." She described this as "imposter syndrome," which is when you don't believe that you are as competent as others think you are. Many women subscribe to it. I have a different perspective. What I believe is really going on is "suppression syndrome," that's when you conceal what you're capable of out of fear of being criticized. You hide who you are because you don't know how other people will perceive you. You know exactly what you want, but you've settled for safety for so long that you've begun to accept it as the norm. And although you feel there's more you can do, you are afraid of the potential judgment you may face.

Do you know why so many states began adopting the "Good Samaritan" law? It's because when bystanders attempted to give life-saving CPR, lawsuits began popping up all over the place from people claiming that their ribs were broken or the chest compressions caused other bodily damage. So, what naturally happened? People stopped being willing to perform CPR, even though they had the skills to step in and save a life. They suppressed it because they didn't want to be sued. Think about that for a second. If you knew CPR and saw someone on the ground and they weren't breathing, would you wait for someone more "qualified" than you to swoop in and save the day? No, because you know, doing something...anything would increase their chances of survival. You'd step in and give them CPR.

The "Good Samaritan" laws were created to protect those who helped another in a real emergency, life-or-death situation from liability. That is what grace does for you. It gives you permission to see a need and know that you have what it takes to fulfill it. You are hesitant to go for it when it's time to do something that may not warrant the validation you've grown used to because you're afraid of deviating from the formula and disappointing other people. It's not because you're not capable; it's because you want to avoid the backlash that comes from it when you do. We learn that early too.

Punt, Pass & Kick

I remember rolling past a giant banner plastered across a Mac truck, and it read, *NFL presents Punt, Pass & Kick*. My parents, who were apparently in no hurry to get home, agreed to pull over.

"Can we pleassse stop?" My little brother begged as he rolled down the window of the car.

Deep down, my dad was equally as eager and as curious as my little brother, who was an up-and-coming pee wee Minneapolis Parks and Recreation football star. This was too good an opportunity for the young phenom to put on a show in his mind.

As the registrar would explain, "Punt, Pass and Kick" was a "skills competition for children ages 6-15 that allowed each contestant to execute each of these areas and then be placed for prizes according to their total score." She hinted that there was a possibility that "the winner could be featured on the news, and perhaps even an NFL player would stop by to survey the fresh talent."

The ink from my dad's signature wasn't done drying on the signup sheet before the sentence finished escaping her lips.

"And what about you?" she said, turning to me. "Would you like to register too"?

I scanned the field and could not find one other girl. She must have sensed my hesitancy and added, "It's just for fun."

"Humph" was my initial response.

She didn't know that nothing was ever "just for fun" in our household. Although at first, I played coy, 11-year-old me was nothing to mess with. So, this was a chance to compete with and beat my brother, and there were bragging rights involved. Always up for a good challenge, I accepted her offer and headed towards the field.

They gave the group instructions and a few minutes to practice, and then it was on! First up was the punt, and I nailed it! Next up, the pass. I stepped up to throw the ball and could hear the crowd going wild in my head. Part of me started picturing the possibility of being the first girl in the NFL. Then I walked up to the kick confidently...womp womp womp...it veered way off to the left. Those same cheers in my head turned into boos, snapping me out of my brief fantasy. Suddenly I realized that the boos weren't actually in my head. They sounded familiar and were accompanied by a taunt.

"Get her out of there. She sucks."

I turned around to see who had the audacity to say that, especially in front of my dad. But much to my surprise, as my eyes scanned and then locked in on the critic in the crowd, I realized the familiar voice was my dad! As a daddy's girl, I was so disappointed. Crushed and crying uncontrollably, I covered the embarrassment on my face with my hands and ran off the field. You would have thought someone inflicted physical pain. I flung myself into mom's arms. Visibly upset but never once losing an ounce of composure, she scooped me and walked me to the minivan. As we waited for my brother to finish, we both stewed in silence, occasionally broken up by my hyperventilated breathing from crying so hard.

As my father and brother made their way back to the car, I could see my brother happily recapping his experience and showing off the trophy he had won from doing so well. He got in the car, but before he had the chance to boast, he could feel something was off.

"What's wrong with you?" he asked, seeing my face but oblivious to what just went down. No one said a word. He shrugged, continuing to admire his new hardware for the rest of the silent drive home.

When we got home, my mom motioned my dad to hand over the car keys and unmuted herself.

"Get back in the car." She instructed me with a firm yet calm tone.

She circled the van, hopped in the driver's

seat, and patted the front passenger seat, summoning me next to her. She pulled me close, our eyes affixed, and said, "You can do anything you put your mind to!"

This was a mantra she said to my brother and me often. But this time was different. This time was one of those Mama Moments. You know, one of those occurrences you never forget. She continued drilling me with passionate encouragement and an uncharacteristic force, unusual of her calm and gentle nurturing self. I can't remember *exactly* what she said after that, but I imagine it looked something like the poetic pep talk Chris Gardener (played by Will Smith) delivered to his son in the movie, *Pursuit of Happyness*:

> *"You got a dream, you gotta protect it. People can't do something, can't do somethin' themselves, they wanna*

tell you you can't do it. If you want somethin' go get it. Period."

By the time she wrapped up her speech, we had arrived at the same field from earlier that day, staring at the sign that summoned us to "Punt, Pass, and Kick" in the first place.

"Try again," she urged. "This time without any distractions."

I gave it another try, placing higher than my baby brother and keeping my silent promise to prove him wrong. Even though I didn't get discovered as the next football great or become the first girl to go to the NFL, I got some serious bragging rights and a glimpse of what I was capable of achieving.

Anticipate that along the way, people may doubt you, your abilities, and even your desire. It can be hurtful enough to make you reconsider what you want to pursue, especially when it comes from the people you least expect. With the invention of social media, criticism will even come from complete strangers.

So, how do you sift through these assessments? *Eat the morsels that apply and leave the rest of the meal.* Filter where it's coming from. If it comes from a negative and not constructive place, then know it probably has less to do with you and is more about how they feel or think about themselves or even view the world. Perhaps they're trying to protect you. They may be trying to warn you of danger, calamity, or mistakes. Or they could be downright trying to dissuade you from achieving your goals. Also, know that sometimes the people sitting on the sidelines of your life may genuinely want to see you win. However, they are simultaneously scared because they just can't visualize that what you want is possible, especially if it hasn't been done before.

Most people don't know what to do with that.

Like Brene Brown says in her book, *Dare to Lead*, "If you're not in the arena getting your ass kicked, then I am not interested in your feedback!" The bottom line is it's easy for people to talk about what they would be doing if they were in your shoes. But if they're not, then it is just that, TALK!

As women, we've come a long way, but we're still experiencing a lot of firsts, even now. I also have to acknowledge that as black women, historically, our people have had to be more concerned with survival and safety, which is secondary to success or self-actualization. However, others' fears are not a reflection of what *you* are capable of; it's simply an indicator of what they're comfortable with. That's called Hegemony.

What the Heck is Hegemony?

I did not learn this "fancy" word until years after the football incident, but I immediately recognized it correlated with what I felt that day. My English professor, Dr. Davenport, had us spend an entire semester exploring hegemony and recognizing its role in our personal and professional pursuits. The term hegemony, created by Marxist thought leader, Antonio Gramsci, is defined as the dominance of one group over another by imposing ideology. It's the way our culture was intentionally created.

The way that hegemony works is that we're spoon-fed social norms through education, sports, religion, family, and the media. We slowly digest what is and isn't acceptable based on others' reactions until it becomes common sense or just the way things are.

The messages aren't always blatant, clear, or as loud as my dad was that day at football camp. Most of them are very subtle suggestions. Whether you are aware of it or not, they have shaped your life in one way or another. You've learned to abide by rules that were in play long before you were born, rules that cause you to contort, conform, and comply without question in exchange for approval. This is important because until you understand what you've been taught about how to survive and succeed in society as a woman, you will continue to operate on autopilot.

The Power of Patterns

Let's take a quiz.

All you have to do is answer the following questions:

1. For breakfast, I like two eggs, bacon, and a slice of ____.
2. I like to spread butter and jam on my ____ in the morning.
3. What do you put in a toaster?

Was your answer to number three toast? If so, you were incorrect. The correct answer is bread. Toast is what you get out of a toaster, and bread is what you put in. Although you know the answer is bread, the trick question sets you up. You could even say you were set up for failure.

Here is the trick; I prepped you with two statements where the correct answer was toast, and those two questions created a pattern that your brain recognized. Once the pattern was established, your brain took over and did the rest. This resulted in an immediate, yet incorrect, response to the question.

That is how hegemony works.

Your actions are almost always based on the patterns and habits you've learned, many of them from childhood. From there, we drag these habits into our adult lives, potentially causing us to settle for the most commonly held beliefs about what life as a woman is supposed to look like, allowing hegemony to dictate our destiny. Hegemony is designed to taint our ambition, steal our perseverance, and cause us to forfeit our tenacity.

What have you been taught directly and indirectly about being an ambitious woman?

- Women must work incredibly hard to become a boss. (In most cases, harder than men).

- Women should bear, raise, and nurture their children. There is guilt implied for not being available to your kids 24-hours a day.

- If a woman leaves her job or career, she may become a martyr for choosing motherhood and family.

It's not hard to see how these perceptions wouldn't make any woman at least a little more cautious when going after what she wants is presented as a high-stakes game. But that is *precisely* what they're designed to do. These and so many more ideals all orbit around the same notion; a woman cannot have the best of both worlds and must sacrifice one for the other. We're taught to subscribe to the **or** instead of the **and**.

- I can be a good wife and mom **or** have a wildly successful career, vs. I can be a good wife and mom **and** have a wildly successful career.

- I can be passionate about my work, **or** I

can make a profit, vs. I can be passionate about my work, **and** I can make a profit.

On the surface, you know that simply isn't true. However, being repeatedly told and shown this perspective unconsciously causes us to integrate it into the narrative of our lives, allowing everything and everyone else's ideals to have authority over our own. Be honest as you answer these questions.

- Do you feel guilty for not being available to your children 24/7?

- Have you ever held back on pursuing an opportunity simply because you believed it would interfere with or cause inconvenience to your family?

- Have you ever decided not to push for something you wanted because you didn't want to be viewed as problematic?

- Do you hold your tongue when you have

something to say because you don't want
to step on anyone's toes?

The Girl Box

We quickly learn to conform to characteristics
we hope will keep us from being criticized. The
following adjectives describe the attributes and
behaviors frequently used to define acceptable and
expected behavior for "good girls."

Nice	Kind	Loyal
Thin	Sweet	Patient
Quiet	Nurturing	Calm

These carry forward into womanhood and keep us
nicely tucked into our "Girl Box." Abiding by these
characteristics may feel safe and even beneficial
in the short term but are very limiting and cause

liabilities for your life in the long term. They function like an invisible electric fence keeping you within their boundaries and shocking you back in place when you step outside the box. They can sometimes even keep you from ever exploring anything outside of their limits because even the anticipation of the shock is so great that you don't even attempt to see if it's something you can handle. That is the point; to keep you on the sidelines of your goals and dreams, to keep you boxed into the ideals that others have for the way you live your life, and to make you settle for the life that was crafted for you instead of intentionally creating the one that you've been called to!

Whenever you are demeaned, insulted, called a name out of character, or even slandered because you have stepped out of the "girl box," the intention is to shock you back into place. When you are paid less than your male colleagues for the same work, that is designed to remind you of *your place*. When you are reminded of what you could lose by pursuing your dreams, that too is a tactic to control your behavior and encourage you to stay within the boundaries of the "good girl box."

How to Fight Back

Women's boxing champion Laila Ali fought back against these very ideals and expectations of girls' boxing. At age 7, she first told her dad, boxing legend Muhammed Ali who converted to Islam in 1964 and put everything on the line for his religion, that she "didn't want to be a Muslim." Can you imagine the courage it took to say this? Of course, as a kid, she didn't fully grasp the gutsiness of saying it.

"It just didn't feel natural to me. And I felt like whatever is in my heart is in my heart. I don't care how old I am," Laila admitted.

Ten years later, she took a stand, exiting the religion chosen for her and embracing one of her own. Her father was both disappointed and angry but eventually accepted her choice. However, that battle wouldn't be their last. At the age of 19, Laila decided that she wanted to box. Many assume it was because she wanted to follow in her father's footsteps, but she was actually inspired by seeing other women in the boxing ring. Knowing her father would disapprove, she began training in secrecy. When he found out what she was planning on doing, he heavily discouraged it because he felt like it was something that "women didn't do."

"What's going to happen if you get knocked down?" he asked.

Laila's response was the type of response, so many of us wish we would have had the courage to say at some point in our lives. She rebutted her dad with, "Well, if I get knocked down, I'm going to get back up, just like you did."

She second-guessed herself a few times, but she decided to go for it after doing some soul searching. Despite the doubters, she defeated some of the most prominent names in women's boxing and retired with a 24-0 winning record. Seeing her success in the ring unleashed the revelation that no role or label could define her unless she allowed it to. She transferred her championship mentality into motherhood and business.

Shortly after her father died, she asked her mom, "Do you *really* think daddy was *really, really* proud of me?"

Her mom responded, "Yes, your dad *really* was proud of you. You changed his mind about boxing and women in sports....and that was big because you know your father; he was very hard-headed."

My Dad is one of my biggest cheerleaders. Our "come-to-Jesus" moment and a tough conversation became the catalyst to me playing basketball, which until this day makes him very proud. If you want to change the game, not only for yourself but for the generation of girls that come after you, you've got to be willing to confront the consensus of how things have to be. This is how we liberate ourselves! As Marianne Williamson pointed out in her poem, Our Deepest Fear, "When we are liberated from our own fear [of criticism, failure, and perfection], our presence automatically liberates others to do the same."

You may have been handed a game plan, which has gotten you far. Thank goodness for that grace, girl! Despite the many messages you've received about how you should operate based on the approval, applause, and acceptance of others, you still crave authenticity. And that is precisely what's possible when you choose not to allow the thoughts, attitudes, ideas, and beliefs of anyone to keep you boxed in.

Laila Ali is a classic case study of what's possible or what it's like to live un-boxable. When you choose not to let the thoughts, attitudes, and beliefs of anyone keep you bound, you fear regret more than you fear failure. You refuse to try to fit in, and you're willing to confront the way you feel things have to be according to someone else's measuring stick. You are ready to stake your claim to the life *you want* to live and by *your own* standards.

Space for Grace

We've all been culturally conditioned to believe that we had to follow the rules to be liked, accepted, safe, and successful. That's not your fault, but it is your responsibility to break free. It's time to get rid of the rules. You have to strip away the things you have been taught about your limitations and start to ask yourself the straightforward question, "Is this true about me?"

What rules have you learned regarding what to do and what not to do? Write them in the **Do Rules** and **Don't Rules** columns below. I've given you some examples to get started. What rules do you need to unlearn or redefine? When you exemplify the bravery of breaking barriers, it offers other women the grace to do the same.

Do Rules	Don't Rules
• Be Strong • Be Perfect • Be what I want you to be • Suffer in Silence • Stay Busy • Clean your plate • Be Successful • Hustle Hard	• Don't Make Mistakes • Don't Fail • Don't trust yourself • Don't break the rules • Don't talk too loudly • Don't brag • Don't break family traditions

Chapter

What's Diet Got to Do with It?

"To continue to live in this body and survive in this body and be happy and actually enjoy life, I need to find a way to like myself."

-Lizzo

*E*very day you push our minds and bodies to the limits, but we don't take the time to train our bodies to accommodate the load. We've been taught to look at our bodies as objects and for the pleasure of others. We've been taught to be ogled and ostracized instead of powerful temples that house our potential.

A prime example of this at the highest level is Serena Williams. She is one of the most successful tennis players ever to play the game, but her dominance is still sometimes overshadowed by her physique.

She's been told that she belongs in "men's sports." Eventually, she says, "I embraced it, realizing that this is me, and this [her body] is my weapon and machine."

Sheesh! That is an entirely different way of viewing your body; as a weapon and machine. How much more powerful would you move through the world if you view your body as a weapon, focusing on how it functions and feels versus how it is seen? You would probably clothe her differently, treat her differently, and feed her differently.

I know this isn't typically what you'd find in a book about business, but I also understand that the way that you view your body can be a barrier in your business. So, that's why we need to talk about it. The relationship you have with your body and the food you eat can give you insight into how you pursue your most meaningful goals.

We restrict based on how we believe things have to be, and when that doesn't work, we give up and binge to make ourselves feel better. It shows up in small, subtle ways, like going all-in on a diet before a wedding or a vacation but going right back to our old overeating habits once the event is over. We follow this vicious cycle in many detrimental ways that numb what we really want. It's a form of perfectionism, the kind that can paralyze you. We tell ourselves:

- If I can't be the best, then I'm not even going to try to do that.

- If I can't work out for an hour, then I'll just skip the whole thing

- Either I am a success or a failure

When we don't feel good about our bodies, we don't allow people to see us. We hold back. That means there are opportunities that we want but don't go after because we're worried about how other people will see us. It's called Social Physique Anxiety (SPA). SPA is a particular form of anxiety that refers to the discomfort experienced when people feel that their body is being evaluated by other people in some sort of social situation. Can you think of a time when this happened to you? Perhaps you didn't go to a party because nothing fit quite, right. Or do you struggle with making yourself visible; so no one knows that your company exists? Maybe your kids wanted you to take a swim with them, but you couldn't enjoy the moment because all you could think about was how you'd look in your bathing suit. Even the thought of standing up in front of a group giving a presentation makes you sick.

SPA is so common that when we come across a woman who doesn't fit the "traditional" body type, but she exudes confidence when she walks in a room and steals the attention, she leaves you scratching your head about what she has that you don't. Nothing! She's simply not playing the game or at least not letting it keep her on the sidelines.

When your primary focus is on the way you look, you will do whatever it takes to have the physical appearance you want, even if it doesn't feel good and even if the moment is short-lived. I learned this when I entered my first fitness competition. The process was grueling. I did cardio 2-hours a day some days. The caloric deficit was so crazy; I passed out. The occasional smell of pizza once made me cry because that's how badly I wanted a slice. While I ended up looking AH-MAZING, there was no way that I could sustain it. It was too extreme. Remember, path #2. I'm a go-hard girl, but it has always come at the expense of consistency. This all-or-nothing mentality kept me "yo-yoing" in my body and business for more years than I care to count.

Instead of having compassion for ourselves, it results in a loop of guilt and shame. Then we turn back to food for comfort, convenience, or punishment.

Have you noticed that I haven't once mentioned the word weight? That's because This isn't about the weight. It's about the actions and habits that cause us to stuff our feelings and restrict our desires. Weight is the side effect of what's happening in our minds. So many of us struggle with it.

Seventy-five percent of Americans are overweight, 67.8% are women. This tells me that there are a lot of us dealing with this issue. Even if it is not your situation, or you struggle with the flip side of this coin, the idea of feeling like you have to work for your worthiness based on your appearance still applies. In her book, *Women Food & God*, Geneen Roth says, "We think we're miserable because of what we weigh. But if we've spent the last five, twenty, fifty years obsessing about the same ten or twenty pounds, something else is going on. Something that has nothing to do with weight." And that happens in all sizes.

It has become yet another way that "shrink" us into something we see as more acceptable before we can have the life we want. The struggle stems from the same mindset, and it often doesn't come from a true desire to be healthy. This isn't about what we eat, as much as it is awareness about why we eat.

In the movie, Self-Made, Madam C.J. Walker's story, the first black female millionaire in America. I couldn't help but notice the scene where she anxiously awaited a visit from Booker T. Washington to endorse her business she picked at the food on the table. When he didn't show up, she sat down and consoled herself with a full plate of food instead of dealing with what she was really feeling; disappointment. We later learn that she passed away as a result of hypertension.

I was definitely eating my emotions when I would binge going in on the hotel gift store snacks. I was bound for a breakdown with the amount of potato chips, ice cream, candy, and coffee I consumed. You can't put gasoline in a diesel engine; doing that would ruin it. We can't put junk in our bodies and expect optimal performance. We also can't withhold nutrients from it and expect it to grow. Pursuing something bigger than yourself can be stressful, lonely, scary, riddled with rejection, and plain ole' hard. When you go to reach for something to eat in one of those moments, ask yourself:

- Am I really hungry?

- Why am I reaching for that?

- What is it that I am really feeling right now?

Once you've realized that it's not necessarily food you're craving, the next step is figuring out what you're hungry for. I can bet it's for a little bit more kindness, self-love, acceptance, and of course, grace [for yourself]. Remember, it's not about all or nothing. Even if you find that you are actually hungry for a slice of pizza or occasional chocolate chip cookie, it won't undo all of the work you've done. It's the small changes that add up to significant improvements in your lifestyle.

Space for Grace

Become best friends with your body! This isn't an overnight process, but accepting and appreciating her (your body) for what she's already done for you will take you farther than hiding and hating her. Create three performance-based goals for your body.

Performance-based goals (PBG) allow you to focus only on what you can control. For example, instead of making it your mission to lose 20 lbs, make the goal to work out three times a week. If you show up to do the work every day, the outcome is inevitable. No matter the outcome, the progress achieved cannot be denied. You will get better and be that much closer to your goal. Note you can apply the same approach to your business.

What are your performance-based goals?

PBG #1 _____

PBG #2 _____

PBG #3 _____

Chapter

What to Expect When Expanding

Everybody has a
until they get Plan
has a plan

"Everybody has a plan until they get punched in the face."

-Mike Tyson

until they get
punched in the
until they get
in the face

99

**Twinkle Twinkle Little Star. How
we wonder what you are!**

This favorite childhood nursery rhyme inspired the theme for our gender reveal party. We were meticulous planners. We waited five years into our marriage to have a child because we wanted to be ready. We wanted things to be right. We wanted to be financially stable, give ourselves ample time to live as a married couple, build stable careers, etc., and when we felt we were close enough, we pulled the trigger.

Now, here we were, surrounded by twenty of our closest colleagues, family, and friends, all crammed into our apartment eagerly awaiting the news on the gender of our first child. Family members who could not be present hung out on a phone tree while taking bets on whether we were having a boy or a girl. My husband and I clasped the handle of the cake knife, cuddled together; the same way we did on our wedding day. We excitedly prepared to cut into the cake that contained the most anticipated answer of the day. As we nervously sliced through the thick fondant, what I already knew in my gut was about to be revealed. Two slits unveiled layers of pink frosting, and just like that, it was confirmed, we were expecting a baby girl. I jumped into my husband's arms, ready for this next phase in our lives.

As the evening began to wind down, we escorted

our guests out as they said goodbye. There were a few stragglers who hung around and joined me to watch the premiere of Beyonce's documentary, *Life is but a Dream*. Anyone who knows me knows I love all things, Bey! I was mesmerized by her story as she shared the painful experience of the miscarriage of her first child. After she finished telling her story, she sang the lyrics,

> *"You took the Life Right out of Me. I'm so unlucky. I can't breathe. I'm longing for your heartbeat, heartbeat."*

There was something about the way she bellowed out the words. There was a pain in her voice that only a mother would recognize. I immediately cradled both sides of my stomach. "I can't imagine having to go through anything like that," I said aloud.

Later that evening, as I was getting ready to go to sleep, I attempted to slip off my wedding rings the same way I did each night before bed. However, this time, I could not get them past my knuckle. My fingers had swollen to the size of Vienna sausages. I presumed this was all part of being pregnant, and it would be the first sign of things to come; little did I know.

During a follow-up meeting with my Obstetrician a few days later, I mentioned the recent symptoms I was experiencing. In addition to my swollen hands, my feet had begun to swell, and I began having severe headaches, which were so bad, I could not tolerate the light while watching television.

> "That's a normal part of pregnancy," she attempted to assure me as she scribbled on her prescription pad. She ripped the prescription from her notepad and handed me her remedy for my symptoms, prescription-strength Tylenol.

"Could it be preeclampsia?" I asked, a little unnerved, as I recalled a pregnancy book I had previously read. My symptoms resembled those described in the book, every one indicated preeclampsia.

"It's too early," she responded. I was 20-weeks along. "Take the Tylenol and give me a call if things get worse."

Well, worse, they got. A few nights after our visit, a sharp pain lit up my spine while in bed, and I shot straight up in my bed, shaking my husband awake.

"We need to go to the hospital now!" I urged.

They ran test after test at the hospital and could not seem to find any issues.

"Maybe we overlooked a bladder infection," the doctor discussed with the nurse.

They ran a check for it, but what they found was something more severe and sinister to the health of my unborn child and me. As it turned out, I, in fact, had preeclampsia. But even worse, it had escalated into HELLP syndrome.

The symptoms I was experiencing were spot on with this condition. My ballooned hands and feet, the blinding headaches, the dots dancing across my eyesight, and elevated blood pressure were all a melting pot of symptoms, representing preeclampsia. Then, stacking HELLP syndrome on top of the preeclampsia triggered my body to begin to shut down. My kidneys began to fail, which explained the pain I felt in my back. My blood platelets drop to their lowest levels. Because of my low blood count, any ideas of having a cesarean were now out of the question. Both illnesses caused my blood to thin, which meant that any cut to my abdomen would cause me to bleed to death; another symptom of preeclampsia was my blood's inability to clot.

I felt like I was in a boxing match with my own body. I felt betrayed by it and by my Obstetrician. I specifically asked about preeclampsia but was dismissed without any investigation. Nonetheless, my husband and I were now faced with making quick decisions in the heat of the moment. Although I was in excruciating pain and my body was taking a severe beat down, I still tried to bargain for options that would afford me more time to nurture the growing child in my womb. How long could I hold out, with the pain, to give my baby time to develop? What else could be done to stop the illness from progressing? I was desperately seeking a way to sustain myself in this situation.

My questions were abruptly interrupted by the stern voice of the Obstetrician warning, "If you don't deliver this baby now, you are going to die!"

His words were a body shot that knocked me off my feet. I was dazed, delirious, and semi-consenting to all that needed to be done but still not quite comprehending what was happening. The pace quickly picked up around me. The nurses buzzed about, adding Pitocin to my IV drip to speed up the birthing process. Yet still, I desperately clung to the hope that my underdeveloped baby would be OK. Maybe God is using me to perform a miracle. I am obedient. I have tried to do things the right way. There is no way that this could be happening to me! So, I squeezed each drop of doubt out of my mind and clung to my lifeline of hope.

Suddenly I felt the urge to push. One push, and she slipped right out, still beautifully packaged in the amniotic sac. McKenzie, my first baby girl, was born asleep at 20-weeks, too small to survive.

The nurses cleaned her up and placed the delicate miniature replica of my husband in my arms, wrapped in a tiny blanket. As I held her, I searched her face and found a resemblance to his nose, eyebrows, and lips. Her little toes, hands, and other body parts were fully formed. And then, in an instant, a switch flipped in me, and the light, the realization of what was happening, hit me hard. The baby I was holding was lifeless and limp. I began wailing. I could not help but wonder what had gone wrong. What did I do to deserve this? My heart shattered into a million pieces, and so did my self-perception. While I knew I didn't do anything wrong, and this was all out of my control, it didn't stop me from blaming myself. I instantly learned the tendency to self-criticism.

I realized how unprepared I was. Up until that point, I hadn't really gone through much. I thought that being blessed meant that nothing bad would happen. I felt that if you just did the "right" thing, that tragedy or hardship wouldn't happen to me. I thought that somehow God would spare me from the tough times. Well, He's not a genie. When things don't go according to our plans, it can leave a crack in your confidence and a fracture in your faith. I was walking around with superficial faith, and when you don't have a real relationship with God to anchor, that is what makes it so hard to come back from life's inevitable defeats.

If you've ever seen the movie, Enough, then this is the part where I pull you in close like Slim's (played by Jennifer Lopez) martial arts trainer and tell you:

> *"...The hardest lesson is that we can't control the universe... To win, we must prepare even for the impossible."*

It isn't the tough times that defeat us; it's our lack of preparation. It's when we expect everything to happen with certainty that we let our faith falter. Knowing that obstacles will arise, we have to be prepared for them. The foundation of preparation is faith. Getting through the tough times requires going from superficial to substantial faith, recognizing that there are times, situations, and circumstances that are sometimes just beyond our control. Yet, you act with such conviction that you're willing to move without tangible proof that things will work. Scripture says, "walk by faith and not by sight."

There is always something beautiful on the other side of your pain. Stop trying to avoid it. As painful as it is, when one part of you dies, another part of you is reborn.

Space for Grace

Carve out some time to get to know yourself. What are your strengths, skills, weakness? Most of us have been taught to look outside ourselves for the answers to our questions, so when something comes up and we have a gut feeling, we don't know how ize our intuition. Our gut is how God speaks to us, so it's important to establish a practice and routine that allows you to look inside. That gut feeling will help you make better decisions, solve problems, and unleash your creativity. You can download a complete guide for creating a morning routine: https://rashidamckenzie.lpages.co/master-your-morning.

Chapter

You Need It All

**When events occur
that we don't expect,
they increase our faith,
strengthen our ability to
endure, and bring forth
hidden talents, abilities,
and strengths.**

-Iyanla Vanzant (Acts of Faith)

*E*xactly ninety days from the date of my loss, I found myself staring at a positive pregnancy test for baby #2. To say that I was terrified would be an understatement! That's the thing about loss; it tends to make you think of the worst-case scenario. I didn't tell anyone that I was pregnant out of fear that something would happen again. At 18-weeks pregnant, I scheduled an appointment with my OB following a gut feeling. I wanted to confidently share the news with my family and make sure everything was alright before we got on the road for our annual Thanksgiving trek to my grandmother's house in South Carolina. I thought it would be a pretty routine ultrasound. They'd check the size and growth of the baby, how the pregnancy was progressing overall, and I'd be on my way. The nurse did the ultrasound, and then my doctor came in.

"Do you feel that?" He asked me.

"Feel what?" I responded.

"Oh! There goes another one! Do you feel that?" He asked again, slightly confused at my lack of reaction to the pain.

"No!" I said, confused and now scared.

"You're having contractions, and you're two-centimeters dilated."

I was in utter disbelief. *Not again*, I thought.

Being faced with the possibility of back-to-back devastation after you've just recovered from one is like realizing you've been standing on quicksand. You can worry and work yourself up, which you know will cause you to sink. Or just take a deep breath, get still until you rise above it. The second-time-around you are armed with new insight, information, and intuition.

Intuition comes in many forms, like goosebumps, that *heeby jeeby* chill you get when someone is in your space, a sense of discomfort or unfamiliarity. It can also be an inaudible voice telling you to move, go, or stop. Our instincts are internal instructions, signaling our fight or flight responses. It's there to protect us, yet we find it so easy to ignore as we have become more evolved. We relinquish expert status to everyone. We convince ourselves that education (what we can see and prove) always trumps intuition (what we feel but can't explain). Don't misunderstand me. Years of studying in any area definitely make someone knowledgeable and expert on a topic, but no one has a Ph.D. from **"YOU**-niversity." You are the expert on yourself. The tweaks, the twangs, the crooks, and the cracks are all telling you something. The things that inspire, disappoint, anger, turn you on, turn you off are all keys to unlocking who you are. So, when you're in the process of bringing an idea from conception to completion, you want to work with someone who sees you as a partner, not a pawn.

Regret comes from relinquishing who you instinctively and authentically are to someone outside of yourself. You have got to refuse to be a bystander in your own life. Sometimes even I wish there was a formula, prescription, or path. But nothing in life is one size fits all. You are going to have to feel your way through. But that's the beauty of a partner. They can guide you through based on where you want to go.

Progress Principle

After a bumpy surgery, we were in a holding pattern to prevent my second baby's premature birth. The next 24-hours would determine if I could get back to business or if my cervix's disturbance would cause my water to break anyway. Giving birth at this time would undoubtedly be too soon for my little girl to survive. I waited for the time to pass, like the sand in an hourglass. As I celebrated each passing milestone of the day, I thought we were out of the woods. However, after the waiting was over, my doctor informed me that, while the surgery was a success, the trauma was a lot worse than she'd anticipated. I believe she knew that I would not be going home right away at the time of the surgery, but she did not want to alert me to that. She understood the power of the progress principle: even a small win provides motivation. And the more frequently you experience that sense of progress, the more likely you will sustain in the process.

We're really good at wrapping our minds around guaranteed, short-term goals...what we can get done in 24-hours, a week, or even a month. Most of us struggle with not knowing exactly how long it will take before getting a result. Obviously, this isn't the case in pregnancy. The goal is clear, get to 40-weeks. But unlike you in pursuing your goal, it wasn't that cut and dry for me.

Nonetheless, the underlying fear in both scenarios is the same; the wait (the period in time between when you set out to do something and when it finally comes to fruition.) You want to go from A to Oprah, but you're not considering all of the things, the struggle, the rejection, and everything else she had to overcome in between. You see where she is now and want to get there overnight, and you want it without going through any of the things she went through to get there.

You're terrified of is feeling like all of your efforts may be a waste. What if you do the work, invest the time and energy, and still don't have anything to show for it? That's the devastation you're trying to avoid, especially when you have experienced failure in the past. But instead of anticipating failure and trying to avoid it, you will have to acknowledge that the possibility is there. That is where the power shift occurs in the wait. Facing each situation head-on allows you to proactively respond to potential problems and mitigate complications, come what may in the meantime. Each obstacle on our journey is an opportunity to see that you have the skills to deal with setbacks and to know that you're not being punished. You're being prepared.

Premature Promotion

Contrary to everything you've been taught, there is such a thing as things happening too fast. The promise of becoming an overnight success or a microwave millionaire is being sold everywhere. You've seen this with the promotions plastered all over Facebook. There are testimonies of programs pledging to teach you how to go from a "beginner to a billionaire" in 60-days.

This overnight sensation mentality is far from the reality of the hard work it takes to build and sustain success. Success requires work, process, and steps along a journey that takes you from vision to victory. The point is when you try to skip steps in the process, then you're forced to repeat them. There is no skipping ahead, or there is no going from A to Oprah, as I like to say.

Writing a best-selling book won't happen in a week. You won't build a billion-dollar business before you've banked $50K, and you won't end up in the best shape of your life in six weeks. The faster you keep trying to get there, the more it all starts to unravel. Pace yourself; "steady wins the race." We've seen the damage that microwave success can do. This has been especially prevalent in the overnight sensations we've witnessed in entertainment, most notably over recent years. You can get everything you think you wanted and wished for, only to self-destruct. I call that "premature promotion," when you get what you want but are so busy focusing on the finish line, you neglect the necessary growth that must occur to create something sustainable. I want you to steady yourself. Trust the process and the timeline, and you'll be reaping great rewards in due time. Now, I'm not suggesting that everyone will take years to reach their peak; however, I am saying that regardless of how long it takes, enjoy each step. Stop putting your happiness on hold.

Markers and Milestones

I know how hard it is to be happy about your progress when you can't see the results. It's why you start a 6-month exercise program only to give up 4-weeks into it. Or, you have twenty sales calls, but when you don't get a "yes," after six, you start telling yourself that no one wants what you have to offer. Again, it takes time for the results you desire to appear.

So, how do you stay focused on a goal that's one year or even five years out? By focusing on the next step, baby steps, if you will. The milestones are the reason expectant mothers download pregnancy Apps. We want to track how the baby is growing and developing, and we want to know what is happening from day to day and week to week. We constantly track every detail throughout the process and gain insight into the constant changes.

How often are you tracking the process and progress in your life? Are you happy with the life you've created? Do you feel like you are contributing to the world in the way you want? Are you following through on your promises? Is the person you want to be in alignment with who you say you are? You have to be present and in the moment to answer these questions. Be aware of what's going on.

Goals define where you are going, and milestones let you know where you are. While you are waiting for the fruits of your labor to blossom, you need a reason to stick with it in the short term. We crave immediate feedback that tells us we are on the right path, moving in the right direction. My doctor understood this, and she knew I needed a win mentally.

"We're going to keep you for another two weeks," my doctor decided. Although I didn't like it, it was a milestone I could wrap my mind around and make my way to achieve. This two-week span would bring me to twenty weeks along in my pregnancy, the halfway point. Making it to the halfway point wouldn't make a difference in the outcome, but you know what it did? It gave me the confidence I needed to endure. It gave me something to look forward to. Having the courage to advance; to plow through the fear of what lies ahead is how you create confidence. You become more connected to your core, dreams, needs, and goals as you gain confidence. You have an awareness of what truly fulfills you, opening up a world of possibilities that perhaps you previously shut out.

There is a show called, *I Didn't Know I Was Pregnant.* It's a documentary series about women who didn't know they were pregnant until they went into labor. You're probably thinking, "How is that even possible," right? Well, for most of the women on the show, it is because they'd experienced something in their past that made them believe that it was impossible for them to get pregnant. So, their minds shut out the possibility, causing them to ignore the signs and become disconnected from what's happening inside them. The moment something becomes inconceivable in your mind is the moment that you become disconnected from your purpose.

What goal do you have that seems so far-fetched that it made you believe it was no longer possible? That is the one you need to pay attention to.

I was completely checked out through the first two weeks of bed rest. I even managed to manipulate my mind long enough to feel like I had been checked into a 3-Star hotel. I had access to room service, the food was decent, the staff was attentive, and the silence combined with the blackout shades made sleep sufficient. That delusion was short-lived, and when I woke up, damp, in the middle of the night.

"I think my water broke," I whispered to my sleeping husband. He immediately buzzed the nurse. The test strip test she administered turned blue, indicating it was true; my water had indeed broken. It didn't help that we had to wait a few hours before my Obstetrician would arrive. However, after hours of panicking, it turned out to be a false alarm.

"It was probably sweat, sweetie, " she said sympathetically while simultaneously annoyed with the night nurse.

That test had a reputation for giving false positives, and the nurse ignored the backup method to verify actual results. This was my tipping point, and I could no longer pretend that I wasn't in a hospital. I could not continue to ignore what was happening.

Yet, I was now too afraid to leave. I realized that I would not have this type of care and access at home if something went wrong. And since I was still so far out from delivery, I didn't want to risk it. My mind descended into a downward spiral. How am I going to do this? How could I possibly get from 20-weeks to 40-weeks by myself? Will I be able to work? How am I going to prepare the house for my daughter's arrival? It's incredible how quickly a little turbulence can cause your mind to believe that the whole plane is going down. Perhaps you don't say it out loud, but inside, a tiny part of your mind starts to go there, and you anticipate doom before anything has even really happened.

But we're done with that, right?

The uncertainty of premature labor is no different than the uncertainty of feeling like you're prematurely making decisions. The worry is the same, and the questions are undoubtedly similar.

And the sensitivity of delivering before you're ready is frightening. Here is where having a coach, someone who has been through what you're going through, becomes crucial. Having someone who can help you see a situation for what it is and help you focus on staying present.

The night of my premature labor scare, the nurse on shift would unknowingly become my coach. When she arrived for the evening shift, I was overcome with overwhelm.

"How are you doing?" she asked rhetorically. But the question loosened the dam of anxiety and emotion. Tears flooded my face as I opened the floodgate of all the thoughts floating through my mind. She sat down, held my hand, rubbed it gently, and gave me the advice of a *sage* and *spicy* aunt. In the softest tone, she said, "If you try to skip to the end, then you'll miss what's happening right in front of you. Talk to your baby, sing to your baby, rub your belly, and tell her to stay in there until it's time. Every day that your baby 'bakes' is a gift, so focus on today because that's all you have anyway!" She handed me a tissue to wipe my face and forever shifted my perspective on patience.

I learned that there is no such thing as waiting. There are only the things we do and our thoughts while mustering up patience during the process. What we call "waiting" is in our minds. What's actually happening is you're looking around, comparing your progress and process to other people's. You should, instead, be focusing on your own progress, process, and making and measuring your own milestones. The time is going to pass. Your only job is to do the work. Plant the seed, water it, and get out of the way. When you do, you'll find more peace at your own pace and find a way to produce something positive out of the wait.

She insisted that I stay another two weeks, which

then turned into a total of 8-weeks at the hospital, on bed rest. I was released to go home at 28-weeks pregnant. This was a major milestone as 28-weeks is when a fetus' viability skyrockets, although not officially all-clear for birth. Nonetheless, I decided that I was done worrying. Having a positive outlook and believing you will make it is critical to accomplishing any goal. As we were about to depart, I felt a warmness wash over me, a sense of comfort. Deep within, I knew that we would be ok, and the remainder of my pregnancy was going to be different.

Everything you've been through has brought you to where you are. Don't wallow in discouragement; focus on encouraging yourself through each day. That's all you have anyway.

Space for Grace

You may feel like you should be further along, but when's the last time you've thought about how far you've come. You didn't know it then, but you've needed every experience that you've had up until now. Your story is what makes you unique and unduplicatable. You can create your programs and offerings from this place of awareness and give birth to your big ideas. You realize that you don't have to compare yourself because no one has *your* story.

Using the space below, you're going to create a life map. Draw a line graph that captures your life's high and low points from birth to today. Starting at the left-hand side of the sheet, which represents "birth" (a neutral event), graph the life events and experiences that impacted you by putting them either above the line or below it.

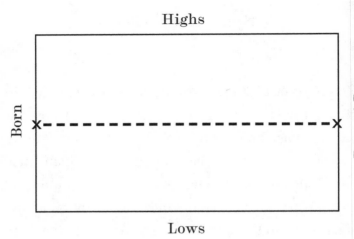

Chapter

Success comes from Structure

"Anything is possible
when you

have the right
people supporting
you

"Anything is possible
when you have the right
people supporting you"

- Misty Copeland

One of the biggest mistakes women often make is forgetting to reevaluate our roles and goals. We fail to adjust to our changes in responsibility. Whether you've gotten married, had a new baby, started a business, or accepted a promotion, so many of us forget to re-align our priorities and renegotiate our contracts.

Before being on bed rest, I took charge of all household duties. I prided myself on not having my husband lift a finger. I planned the vacations and balanced the budget, made home-cooked meals, hosted friends for the holidays, cleaned the house, and, not to forget, performed my wifely duties. However, my doctor had now forbidden me to do a damn thing. All I were to do was eat and rest to hold on to my incubating baby for the next 10-weeks. Telling a Type-A personality to do "nothing for 10-weeks" is like telling a toddler to sit still for 10-minutes; neither will go down without kicking and screaming.

I'm pretty sure the "A" stands for anxiety. The thought of sitting still or even doing the bare minimum bubbled up a level of insecurity and worry that I didn't even know I had. Being in control was my way of calming myself and everyone else down, and here I was, forced to relinquish it without warning.

We constantly stress ourselves to the point of being overwhelmed when we aren't in control, particularly in our homes. In the book *Drop the Ball*, Tiffany

Dufu calls this "home control disease" (HCD). HCD is the desire to feel like everything is controlled and managed in a particular way, your way. We oversee the to-do list down to the most minute details, from the way the clothes are folded and put into their drawers to the brand of OJ we buy for the fridge. There is a nagging fear that things will fall apart if we are not the ones taking care of them. We believe that:

- No one will do it quite as well as we do. You want to ensure that you're indispensable.

- Ain't nobody got time to train other people. You don't want to lose control.

- No one needs to know that you don't have it handled, so we struggle in secret.

- You try to convince others that it only takes a minute, knowing full well that it never works like that and will take you much longer.

- You think you can't afford to delegate (this is a big one) when maybe it's just that you don't really know where to start or what to delegate.

Sure, my biggest [and only] priority was bringing a healthy baby into this world; however, I felt that now that I was home, it was still my responsibility to make sure everything got done. It was a classic case of over-functioning—doing more than is necessary, more than is appropriate, and more than is healthy. In other words, doing way too much! Being extra isn't a bad thing but being extra at the expense of your sanity is self-sabotage.

- Have you said yes to something while knowing you don't have the time?

- Have you ever offered up your help for the sake of conversation?

- Do you jump in and try to fix a problem just because someone shared a problem with you?

The problem is that when you over-function, the people around you inevitably under-function and assume, "she's got this!" knowing eventually that if something is left undone, your inner Olivia Pope will show up sooner or later and handle it. It's easy to get locked into this dynamic because it's hard to break the cycle when everyone gets used to operating that way. Let's be clear it's not about blaming, though, simply recognizing your behavior; because by now, you can probably guess where else this pattern shows up! In your business.

- You overwork on projects without adjusting your rate and then resent the client for taking advantage.

- You overpromise before considering the

time and effort involved.

- You dishonor yourself and show up even when you know you need to be sitting down.

- You don't hire and delegate even when you're drowning in responsibility.

What it all boils down to is worthiness. We tell ourselves that if we're not doing enough, then we're not enough. Well, girl, let me give you some grace. You are loveable, wanted, or worthy just the way you are.

Women have been conditioned to over-function, especially when historically, the home is where women have wielded the most power and gotten high praise. That was also back when keeping a home was considered a woman's primary job and well before we showed up on the work scene and took on the challenge of balancing full-time work with full-time family responsibilities, let alone running a business.

Put your hands in front of your face and cup them together. Despite how much you plan, strategize, or desire, they can hold only so much. Understanding your capacity is a game-changer that allows you to prioritize in a way that leads to significant fulfillment and happiness in your life. Too often, we feel obliged to put everyone else's needs before our own. We wake up each morning in service mode. The children need breakfast, our husbands or partners are leaning on us, and our phones buzz with reminders of our meetings for the day. Topping the mounting strain is the mental load you'll carry through the day as you attempt to multitask between home and work.

Don't underestimate the exchange of energy taking place. No matter how progressive your household is, I'm willing to bet that some adjustments can be made. Michelle Obama has even talked about having some imbalance in the household roles of her and President Obama. However, the dynamic can change if you're willing first to communicate what you need and then open yourself up to seek help outside of your immediate household. During a *Good Morning America* interview, Mrs. Obama shared, "What I learned about myself was that my happiness was up to me, and I started working out more, I started asking for help, not just from Barack [Obama] but from other people. I stopped feeling guilty."

Guilt has to go!

Somehow, *having it all* got mixed up with *doing it all.* Women are sacrificing more than just "me" time in the juggling act of trying to do it all. It's like making lemonade from twice squeezed lemons. What you're left with is a watered-down experience that we attempt to make palatable but don't ever truly enjoy. Perhaps that's you. Have you fallen into the habit of taking on tasks and responsibilities because you believe it's what's expected of you as a wife and mother? Where does that show up for you in your business? So many of us are hesitant to give up the things on our plate, even though they are painful and draining for us to handle. We feel this way, all while knowing that if we were to give them up, not only would it make us more productive, but it would ultimately make us happier.

Still, I fought tooth and nail because I didn't want to feel like I was being a burden. You go hard and help everybody else but won't even allow others to support you without feeling bad about it.

Before my release from the hospital, I spent several days calling around to enlist a company that could provide all of my needs. Much to my surprise, identifying a company of professional support was not as easy as I thought it would be. I called the cleaning companies, but they didn't do laundry. I reached out to laundry companies, and they certainly didn't do any cooking. I contacted catering services, and of course, they didn't clean or do laundry.

There wasn't an Uber Eats, Postmates, Grub Hub, or anything remotely close to that at the time. This prompted me to take out my handy dandy notebook and note these observations. My brain kicked into full gear. *Wouldn't it be helpful if there was a company that could help with it all?* I thought. I was hoping to find a one-stop-shop company to serve all of my needs, but when I couldn't find one, I began to think, *Why don't I just create it?* There had to be other expectant moms, home, on bed rest, and needed help. There wasn't any way I would buy that I was the only one going through this. So, I tucked the idea away in the back of my brain and decided it was time to disrupt the dynamic.

I could not afford any additional stress on my body. The stakes were too high not to shift. I needed to focus, which meant I needed to let go. I constantly heard the nurse's voice in my head, coaching me to do the same. This meant we needed a system that didn't rely solely on me. Out of anticipation of being released from the hospital, I already made a list of all the things I would need help with:

√ Having healthy meals

√ Laundry: Washed, Dried, Folded, and put away 2x week

√ Deep cleaning 1x month.

√ Hair braided so I wouldn't have to do it for a while after having the baby.

I was still under strict orders to stay off my feet, and I even had to sit while in the shower. So, my "job" was to relinquish control! I mobilized my family, friends, and a few familiar services. Everyone had tasks based on what was needed. My Grandma was commissioned to prepare meals. Every few weeks, she shipped a feast via FedEx, which survived on dry ice, and a variation of mouth-watering, home-cooked meals arrived at our doorstep. Did I mention that we live in Maryland, and she's in South Carolina? She's fantastic, isn't she? Whatever she didn't prepare was supplemented by other family or friends who heard about what was happening. Essentially, we created a meal train that meant I didn't have to cook for the remainder of the pregnancy. My husband set up a couch side station for me daily, and he ensured that everything I needed was within arm's reach before he left for work.

My station was fitted with water, magazines, a TV remote, and a fully packed cooler filled with snacks, fruits, and vegetables. He even anticipated my cravings and knew when to slip in a bag of peanut M&M's or gummy worms. I felt like a Queen. Each night he arrived home, he would take care of the dishes without prompting before dozing off to slumber for the night. I hired a husband-and-wife team to clean our apartment bi-weekly, and they kept it in impeccable condition. My mom took care of the laundry, served as the catchall, and pitched in whenever we needed her. The icing on that cake was having my hairstylist make a house call to braid my hair and ensure that would be one less thing I had to worry about when the baby arrived. I was running a well-oiled machine from the comfort of my couch.

When I looked around, my house was clean, smelled like fresh laundry, my belly was full, and my hair was cute. And, after a total of twenty-two weeks of bed rest, I delivered my daughter Maya on my [scheduled] due date full-term and healthy.

When you view support as a superpower and a sign of strength instead of a weakness, the people around you buy-in, and they take ownership of the work and the outcome. They want to see you win! But you've got to be willing to share the load.

Load Management

In 2019, the Toronto Raptors on-boarded NBA all-star Kawhi Leonard. The Raptors had never won a championship, but here they were with one of the league's top players who had the possibility of taking them there. There was only one caveat, Leonard had a lingering injury, and if they weren't careful, it could cancel out not only the season and their run at a championship but his whole career. So, they implemented what is infamously known as "Load Management" to prevent him from re-injuring himself.

In the simplest terms, load management is a holistic approach to lessening the total amount of training and or competition an athlete takes on. The intention is to help them recover and perform better over the long term. For example, in basketball, it's not just about how many minutes you play in the game, but how often you work out practice, travel, and everything else surrounding those game minutes too.

Of course, Leonard's load management made some fans upset. After all, it meant taking a gamble when you'd purchase a ticket and show up at the games because it was a possibility that your favorite player wouldn't be playing. Former players even scoffed at the notion of load management because "back in their day," they sucked it up and played injured and thought he should have too as well!

Just because something has worked for someone else or they have chosen to go about running things differently, it doesn't mean that it works for you or is even applicable to today's world. Whether that's how your mother or grandmother ran their household or the way someone else chooses to conduct their business, you have to understand how to optimize your performance in a way that works for you and find the people who support it.

When Leonard sat out, his teammates stepped up. When Leonard stepped in, he was able to show up and go all out entirely. He led Toronto to their first NBA championship and was league MVP.

I want to support getting you to the place where you can prioritize your wellness without worrying about what those looking on may think.

It can work for anyone, but everyone has to buy into the end goal. Decide where you want to go? What do you need to give up to get the best out of yourself? Develop a daily practice to get there.

As the last week of my maternity leave wound down and I began wrapping my mind about going back to work, my phone rang.

"I really hate that I have to give you this news," the conversation started. From the tone of my caller, I knew it couldn't be good. "Unfortunately," the voice continued. I held my breath as I was told that I was being "laid off." Panic began to set in. *What the hell am I going to do?* I had a new baby, a tired body, and a weary mind. I felt my body welling up with panic. But then, a bolt of enlightenment grounded me. *My notebook!* I began feeling a sense of relief as I remembered the notes I took when I was on bed rest. I pulled it out and reviewed all of my notes from the research I'd done as I was trying to identify a one-stop-shop company that could assist with my household responsibilities. So, I went directly into execution mode and launched a business; with a nine-month-old baby in my lap.

As my business grew legs, the phone began ringing, and the emails poured in. But they weren't from bedridden moms-to-be, the customer I sought to serve. These calls were pouring in from women working long hours, in high profile careers, running their own businesses, having young children, and were overwhelmed and tired of doing it all! Very few of them were carrying a baby, but they were *carrying a mental load*. These women were in "emotional labor." They, too, were in the smoke phase of their lives, a few already in the fire, and were ready to relinquish their household duties. They were worn out from grocery shopping, cooking dinner, running around to pick up the kids from sporting events and birthday parties. They were tired of carpools, mommy-and-me yoga, playdates, party planning, and the smorgasbord of motherly duties expected of them. In Corporate America, this is known as project management. For these women, this was household management, and they were screaming for help. I was the solution.

I began to apply the load management framework

in the homes of prominent female executives and entrepreneurs who found themselves over-functioning and over it. I'll call them Jenna, Nancy, and Emily.

- Jenna, a partner at one of DC's largest law firms handling $50 billion acquisitions. She was working 50+ hours per week and completely exhausted by the time she got home at the end of the day. But it wasn't her work that she wanted to back down from, and it was her second shift that she began each day when she arrived home. Once she accepted that she needed to put out an SOS, she created a strategy from feeling stretched thin and snappy with her family. She wanted to figure out how to relinquish control over some of the micro duties to spend more focused and happy time with her family.

- Nancy, a leader at a top company in Washington, D.C., had dreams of building a speaking and coaching career. A single mom of two teenage sons whose father passed away unexpectedly ultimately put all of the parenting weight on her. With both heavily involved in extracurricular sports, most of her time was spent chauffeuring her children to and from their sporting events. Because most of their time is spent away from home, they lived an on-the-go lifestyle. Their lifestyle directly contributed to their unhealthy eating habits. Fast food, dining out, and snacks-on-the-go were their daily menu. The unfortunate consequence was her health, a clear wake-up call to create a strategy to re-balance her life and her health.

- Emily is a work-from-home consultant

and woman who took pride in the meticulousness of her home for her family. Her home was beautiful and always extremely organized. She ran it a lot like a small hotel. She's a frequent entertainer and very family-oriented. However, the total weight and responsibility of managing such a lifestyle fell squarely on her shoulders. Having had her first child and the desire for another, she often worried about her ability to maintain the same level of dedication to running her home while chasing after a toddler. Additionally, she became increasingly restless about pursuing her dream of becoming a lawyer.

Your situation may be different, but the thread that runs through the stories is all the same: You cannot do it all, and you've already tried that. If you are finding struggle with the juggle, here is where I suggest you start. Start by demolishing your ideas of how things have to be and get clear on what works for you and your family.

Looking at the Big Picture

Have you fallen into the habit of taking on tasks and responsibilities because you believe it's what is expected of you as a wife and mother? So many of us are hesitant to give up the things on our plate that are painful for us to do. Things that we don't even like. And if we gave up, it would not only make us more productive but would ultimately make us happier. We mistake, what I describe as, looking through the little window. This means primarily focusing on the things in our lives that seem small and more manageable, and the consequences are too.

Like laundry, ignoring the pile of stuff in the

middle of the floor, checking email, and grocery shopping all look and feel like the big problem when left undone. Our attention is drawn to the problem instead of the issue at hand. Think hoarders, but in your mind. We see all of the stuff, but deep down, there is something else going on. We just let the little things pile up until they become the big things. So, we never have to face the big stuff. We try so hard to keep people from seeing our mess, thinking that we'll be judged, or people will know that we don't have it all together, so instead of asking for help, we fall into the trap of trying to do everything ourselves. Have you ever said, "By the time I teach someone what else needs to be done, I can just do it myself." Or "What if they don't do it the way that I do it?" Those thoughts are what become the trap.

There is a strategy I use and teach called "Looking at the Big Picture." Imagine a home with big, picturesque floor-to-ceiling windows. They're designed to give you a clear view of your surroundings without any obstructions. The windows create transparency, allowing you to see out and others to see in, but still serve as a boundary between you and everything outside. It's a practice in self-awareness. How much of what you do is being driven by wanting approval and what you want people to see? What would your life look like if you did what's essential, what's necessary, and what's now? Until one day, you get to a place where you can appear in the window without worrying about what other people are thinking. You do that by prioritizing the only four areas of your life that you can't delegate:

Fitness	Family/Friends
Finances	Faith

- **FAITH** – Deepening your connection to your creator is a crucial component to authentic success and, for me, the source of my grace. Grace is simply applying God's unconditional love for us to ourselves and permitting yourself to go after everything God has in store for you. But it is a practice. Having faith means believing in that which you can't yet see with such conviction that you're willing to act on that belief without tangible proof right now. It is the "secret ingredient" that allows you to stop second-guessing yourself and see things through. But it's not something that someone else can give to you. You have to take the time to seek out a real relationship with Him so that you have something to anchor you when life tosses you around. After you've laid out the pros and cons of what you want, it's time to put your faith into practice by creating the space for grace in your day to connect with your creator. Faith is giving yourself permission to go after everything God has in store for you.

- **FAMILY & FRIENDS** - Family and friends are often the people that have the most confidence in you. I know there are exceptions, and some people are just classified as "family by blood," but we're talking about the people in your life that want you in theirs. I combined family and friends because I believe family is what you are given, and friends are your chosen family. These relationships run deep. They sway us, inspire us, and challenge us. They are the ones you draw upon for nourishment, support, and growth. They are the ones who know what it is behind closed doors. They see the insecurities, second-guessing, and your shine. Your closest connections are those who carry your legacy, not the world. The world may get to witness your greatness, but they see the grind. So, make sure you take the time to cherish these relationships. None of what you accumulate can be taken with you when you die. Legacy is what you leave in people, and inheritance is what you leave for people. We'll talk about money in a minute, but it's essential to understand the difference. Because we often work to build a legacy for the world to see. However, success starts and ultimately ends at home. Going back to your inner golden girl. Think about when your grandchildren and great-grandchildren are gathered at your feet; what story of your life will you tell them? What advice will you have for them based on the life you've have lived? You don't want it to be that you were too busy with dishes and errands to do meaningful things.

- **FINANCES** - Knowing how much you need to delegate is part of discovering what you want and where you want to go. Finances undoubtedly help with that (and there is a way to do it even if you think you don't make enough yet.). Now, money can be a conversation women tend to avoid, but you have to get comfortable talking about it. There is freedom in finances, and that is the reality. Nothing kills creativity, joy, playfulness, and peace more than scarcity. How often have you put up with friendships, relationships, or unacceptable situations where scarcity was a factor? It will inadvertently show up in every area of your life and dictate your decisions. In the book, *Self-made* Nely Galán says true financial freedom "means getting out of survival mode, where you are one problem away from catastrophe. It means changing your mindset from instant gratification to goal orientation. It means being able to sleep at night without worry. It means being rich in every way: rich in money, rich in family, rich in love, rich in time— abundant!" Focusing on this area will inadvertently open up your entire life to ease and flow, not to mention your ability not only to increase your income but impact others.

- **FITNESS** - Jim Rohn has been credited with the saying, "You can't hire someone to do the pushups for you." Your fitness level directly affects the building of your legacy because it improves longevity. Do not train for the look, train for strength and endurance. That is how you maximize your potential. You can't deny the demand placed on your body when you're building a business or just trying to keep up with your kids. What good does it do for you to create it but sacrifice the vessel that carried you there? How can you handle growth and expansion if you're too tired and run down to see it through? Don't deny your body what it needs to fuel your dreams.

In the end, no one else is responsible for the life that you've lived or the legacy you hope to leave. So many of us are trying to find balance in figuring out a better way to give ourselves equally to everything, but that isn't possible. You're not seeking balance. What you're searching for is peace. You want to be able to walk through your door at the end of the day without feeling exhausted, defeated, and sad.

Stop comparing yourself to what other women are doing and be comfortable with yourself and your own style. And when you step out of the shower each night and look at yourself completely naked in the mirror and recognize the reflection staring back at you. Indulge yourself in feeling a sense of fulfillment, success, and wholeness that is as beautiful and unique as your body is. However, if you don't feel these senses, then something in you will always feel off.

Start being honest about where you are and where you want to be. When you go through life trying to do it all, you won't have the time and energy to do what matters most. In business and leadership, too many women spend way too much time managing the clock instead of investing in easy and inexpensive options to delegate the micro-tasks. They miss opportunities that will free them up to manage their load. Focus on your career, family, and yourself. Stop using the micro-tasks as distractions.

Have you ever noticed how suddenly you get the urge to organize the pantry when a big project is due? Suddenly, the laundry can no longer wait when you need to follow up with a lead. Don't block yourself from doing the things that move you forward. Stop operating in scarcity, thinking that you can't afford to have help. Think of your life and business as a buffet. You have access to everything laid out when you're at a buffet. However, you also know that you don't need to put everything on your plate to enjoy your experience. Knowing that if you indulged in it all, it would actually create the opposite effect; you'd walk away sick. While buffets are advertised as "all you can eat," no one expects you actually to eat it all. The same holds true in your life. You don't have to do it all, and again, you also don't have to feel guilty for no longer wanting to.

Let me bring you back to Jenna, Nancy, and Emily.

When these women implemented more structure, they were able to experience the benefits of their ultimate goal: Harmony & Freedom. That's really what we're all after. Not balance.

When you have true harmony, what you think, feel, say and do is aligned. When you don't, it shows up as an imbalance - you're irritable, liable to go off over the most minor things, always feel like you're in a rush, you find it hard to make rational calm decisions, and frankly, you feel trapped. This is why harmony and freedom go together and why they flee from our lives as a team. To ensure that these two qualities are present, you need to pay attention to your feelings. The actions that you take should align with the thoughts you're thinking. If you maintain this awareness, you will notice when you are out of harmony. When you detect an imbalance, you are to stop whatever you're doing and investigate where it exists.

- Jenna remained a powerhouse at work but intentionally invested more time with her children, attending games and practices, and taking weekend trips. Some of their vacations were epic memories her kids will cherish for a lifetime. Support became a non-negotiable vs. a nice-to-have, and everyone in her home was happier.

- Nancy helped her boys become more independent, incorporated more home-cooked meals into her routine, and took back control over the health of how her family ate. Additionally, her influence grew at work and in her business. She went up for a promotion, and her business began expanding as well.

- Emily attended law school and landed her dream internship with a firm in Los

Angeles that would launch her career. She even added another little one to the family while doing it.

As the saying goes, "If you don't sacrifice for what you want, then what you want becomes the sacrifice." When you learn to do things with purpose and intent instead of doing them to prove your worth, you propel other people to take responsible action where they need to. There's something powerful about preserving your energy so that you can pounce on new opportunities and push yourself when it's time to. Determine what only you can do and do that!

Despite what you've been told, you don't need to be or appear to be constantly busy to be successful. See success as a measure of doing what matters most to you.

Space for Grace

Allowing yourself to get the support you need is the ultimate form of grace. Let's look at your load and what you can let go of to ensure you stay in the game. I've created a list of some things you might do daily, weekly, or monthly. You can add more activities as you think of them. No task is too small.

In the "Who" column, write the name or initials of someone who can contribute to your team's success and share the load. Here's a hint, it can be a company, and don't forget to include the kiddos.

Who	Activities
	Clean the Bathroom
	Create Documents
	Give the Kids a Bath
	Homeschool
	Laundry
	Marketing
	Meal Prep
	Pack Lunches
	Plan Birthday Parties
	Post on Social
	Potty Train
	Research
	Unload the Dishwasher

Chapter

You're not Starting from Scratch

"Don't be afraid to start over. This time you're not starting from scratch, you're starting from experience."

-Biggs Burke

*W*e have all encountered destiny detours. You know, those experiences that you thought detached you from your dream, disconnected you from your desire and made you decide not to look back, at least until now. No one is exempt from the redirection that masquerades itself as rejection:

- Sara Blakely, a self-made millionaire, failed the LSAT twice, then sold fax machines for seven years before hitting it big after creating Spanx ®.

- Twelve major publishers rejected the *Harry Potter* manuscript before JK Rowling's finally found someone to pay attention.

- Issa Rae was told repeatedly that she didn't fit Hollywood's "standard" and couldn't catch a break. So, she created a YouTube series called *The Misadventures of an Awkward Black Girl*. She played the role herself, which ultimately landed her own HBO series, *Insecure*, and multiple production deals.

If you've concluded that you are not on a path you have intentionally chosen, one that doesn't serve your purpose, you've got to let go of the fear of starting over. I know no one wants to feel like a freshman again. It can be intimidating, exhausting, and frustrating, but the foundation is where grace activates. The hard expectations you hold for yourself lessen, not based on capability but experience, allowing yourself the space and the grace to learn.

Grace is what gives you an advantage because it comes with experience, and it's not like you haven't done it before. You benefit from all the mistakes made, the successes you've had, and all of the lessons learned. You bring it all with you. Burning out always presents an opportunity to rebuild – because it is life telling you, you can't continue to operate in the same way. It demands that you do something different, and rebuilding will require you to leave your comfort zone.

Surrendering to come out of your comfort zone is challenging because it usually requires a significant change in your life. Identifying the areas where you are most comfortable, yet need to get out of, involves a period of silence and stillness. If you are anything like me, there is always something to do, so being still is not always easy, but it is necessary. Nonetheless, coming out of our comfort zones can be tricky. It requires us to begin rocking the boat a little. It requires us to overcome the uneasy feeling in the pit of our stomachs. It requires us to resist the urge to turn back to what we've been so accustomed to.

When you feel the inkling of wanting so much more, that is your inner compass pushing you to pursue discomfort. Ignoring it results in procrastination and lower ambition, leaving much of your life uncharted. All of your choices, good or bad, serve you somehow. They either keep you comfortable or move you forward; either way, they are the comforts we hold on to. Why? Because they're familiar, and we'd much rather face what we're familiar with than embrace the unknown. So, what does actively pursuing discomfort look like? Sitting in it every chance you get.

In the book *The 4-Hour Workweek*, Tim Ferris advised his students to take a comfort challenge. The challenge consists of specific tasks to "get out of their comfort zone." One of the challenges prompted them to call at least one potential "superstar mentor" per day for three days. They could email them only after attempting the phone call. I took this challenge, and immediately when I picked up the phone, my stomach churned. I gulped back the knot in my throat, and in its place, I found my voice. First, I asked to speak with bestselling author, speaker, and social media influencer, Grant Cardone. After a couple of vetting questions, I almost talked his secretary into putting him on the phone, but no luck. But after making this first call, I realized I wasn't going to die. Each subsequent call became easier. Was it uncomfortable? Hell yes! However, I did it anyway.

I challenge you to push through the churning in

your stomach, the frog in your throat, the pounding in your heart, and the sweat in your pits because your power is on the other side. Once you can see where you've been holding back, you'll be able to push through it and move toward a life of FREEDOM!

I must warn you that when you do, the moment that you start something new, your mind will be flooded with all the reasons why you can't, or you shouldn't go for it. Don't get caught in the trap of thoughts like these:

- I don't know how I am going to make it happen.

- What do you think you're doing?

- Who do you think you are?

- Am I qualified enough?

- Let me watch before I jump in.

- I'll start tomorrow.

- I need to wait until the kids are older.

- I don't have the money to do this.

- How am I ever going to get the rest of this done by the end of the day?

You can silence your head hecklers when your mind is flooded by asking yourself two questions: What do I have to lose? And what do I have to learn? And listen. When you do that, you'll begin to get the insight you did not have and get inspired to do things you wouldn't naturally do. You'll meet people through what seems like circumstance and coincidence, and doors of opportunity will open that you didn't even know you had.

Leave It All On The Floor!

Amid my slump, I received a call from my best friend asking me if I could play in her first annual charity basketball game. Initially, I tried to come up with every reason why the timing didn't work for me. I justified not going because I was busy running a business, and spending a day or two away seemed detrimental. But deep down, the truth was that I was afraid. I wasn't in the best shape, and I hadn't picked up a ball in so long that the white Nike check on the outside of my basketball sneakers had turned slightly yellow.

Nevertheless, I decided to dust them off and start training for my return to the court. Yes, training! After years of being away from something, I learned the hard way you don't just jump back in and go full speed. Remember, pace yourself.

Only a few years before this invitation, I was asked to play in a co-ed league at a local gym, just for fun. I'd been doing so well in the games that I convinced my husband that he had to come and see me "school some fools" in the championship game. I wanted him to see that I still "had it." The game's pace picked up, and I could feel a tweak creeping up my back leg. Trying to keep up, I ignored it and kept running. I attempted a layup on a fast break, and I heard a pop in mid-air. I dropped to the floor, clutching the back of my leg. My hamstring felt like a tightly wound guitar string that just got plucked. My husband and a few of my teammates hoisted me up like the trophy I was hoping to win and helped me hobble to the car. I ended up being out of commission for the next six weeks, and I didn't pick up a basketball again for another six years.

So, when my best friend called, I decided to go to Atlanta and play in the charity game. Stepping back onto the court at this point in my life felt a lot like freshman year, becoming a beginner all over again. On the day of the game, as I sat on the bench, I heard the hum of the crowd, and butterflies started nervously dancing in my stomach. A bead of sweat escaped my brow and tapped my shoe with my head bowed. The announcer called me to the floor, and before I knew it, it was game time. I took the first shot of the inaugural game, and it ricocheted off the rim. *Here we go!* I thought. I felt myself begin to shrink. As the game picked up, my shot was still off the mark. Then I remembered that there are other facets to my game.

Just because something doesn't work out on your first few tries, it does not mean that it isn't meant for you to succeed. It means that God has a desire to strengthen other areas in your life so that you are prepared to weather the storm. Stop thinking that because one way doesn't work, that means it's the only way. Trust that every single gift you've been given opens up different options for you to seize your opportunity.

I turned up my defense. I began to dive after loose balls, boxing out the offensive players and going after every rebound. My defense resulted in game-changing turnovers, which allowed me to score. The game came to me! Something magical happened, and the buzz of the crowd slowly faded away, and I focused on playing the game *my way*. I was experiencing *flow*.

Flow is a term created by Psychologist Mihaly Csikszentmihalyi. It is often described as a mental state where people experience complete immersion and involvement in an activity. Things seem to happen almost effortlessly, and time seems to disappear while in this state. Athletes often refer to this state of mind as being "in the zone."

The key to finding your flow is doing something that absolutely lights you up on the inside, something that unlocks new levels of focus, productivity, and fun! To fully experience flow, you have to embody your purpose and pursue it relentlessly. You must be willing to take the last shot, to want the ball in your hands as the clock winds down, no matter what happens. The only difference between the good and the great is the willingness to live with the grief that comes from missing the mark and the glory that comes with winning. And doing so without attaching your worth to either outcome.

When you're too afraid to fail or look foolish, you will coast through life and never come close to reaching your full potential. Perfection simply doesn't exist, and you will make mistakes. If you're not failing from time to time in your pursuits, you're not pushing yourself. And if you're not pushing yourself, you're probably not making room for grace in your life or your business. Doing what it takes just to get by is destined to create a list of *shoulda, coulda, woulda's*. Kobe Bryant so eloquently put it like this:

> "Those times when you get up early, and you work hard, those times when you stay up

late, and you work hard, those times when you don't feel like working, you're too tired, you don't want to push yourself, but you do it anyway. That is actually the dream. That's the dream. It's not the destination. It's the journey."

Everything that happens is a by-product of your willingness to scrape your knees, take risks, get knocked down, rebound and repeat. Safe won't get you to your full potential. You must push yourself beyond the boundaries you and others have set and do it with your knees knocking. Leave it all on the floor!

We won that charity game! I stood still, in the middle of the floor on the brink of tears as I breathed in the moment. I surrendered to my greatness that day.

When you go from seeking approval to knowing

that you only need your own, you'll stop asking for permission. You'll stop trying to prove anything to anyone but yourself. When you approach your performance this way, the world gets to witness the culmination of practice, prayer, planning, and preparation that comes together when you dare to be obedient to the call. So, when you finally go for it, you'll appreciate the applause, but you won't need it. You'll hear the crowd, but you won't be distracted by the noise. And you'll want to win but won't waste time worrying about whether or not it will happen. You'll just do the work knowing that it will!

Space for Grace

Now that you're clear on your core values, you're aware of your patterns and societal protocols, and have the benefit of looking back over your life, how do you define success? Why do you want it? Based on how you define it, is there anything you need to do differently to access it? What are you willing to surrender for it?

Remember, you get to define and design it on your own terms this time. Give yourself full permission to dream no matter how wild and crazy it may seem.

Chapter

You Get to Choose

I've been always following people, like, sort of following blueprints of people. And now I feel like I didn't really find or, like, see a lane or a path that I liked, and I was at a standstill. And then I found that you have to make your own path."

- Naomi Osaka

You get to Choose

Ok, so which way do you go?

As you exit the pages of this book, move about in the world, and begin to discover who you are and the path you want to take. Know that you may be the first in your family or circle of friends to decide to pursue your most audacious dreams; a voyager of sorts. But as you navigate the naysayers, something beautiful happens. The fog of doubt, distraction, and discouragement will begin to fade, and you'll start to see your destination off in the distance.

As each layer of that curtain lifts, you'll begin to see that a lot of what has held you back may have started as hegemony but has become habitual. And now you know that habits are changed through intentional choices.

I imagine the first time a snake sheds its skin, it doesn't really know what's going on. All it knows is that being inside of its skin becomes so uncomfortable that it has to find relief. So, it starts to rub up against rough surfaces, hoping to release itself from the skin. Instinctively the snake knows there is a way out! Eventually, it slithers out of its skin, revealing a new layer and leaving the old behind. This is how courage works—taking what has been so familiar to you all your life and shedding the thoughts, ideas, people, and things that no longer work for you. And doing so without knowing where the process will lead you.

Nelson Mandela said, "Courage is not the absence of fear but rather the ability to overcome fear when we want something bad enough." Courage allows you to have those hard conversations with the people closest to you and openly express what this new journey looks like for you. Why? A declaration is a sign of courage. You've got to say it out loud, so someone other than yourself knows. So, when things get tough, you don't go back to shrinking yourself and playing small.

When things begin to change, we tend not to want

to step on anyone else's toes or inconvenience their comfort. We worry more about what other people are going to think of us. Staying in this mindset keeps you stuck in internal torment because you are not being true to yourself.

What are the situations in your life where you are not openly expressing what you want?

You are here because, at one point, you may have chosen the path of least resistance. You did what was comfortable, thinking it would still somehow get you where you wanted to go. Yet, something still wasn't working. You secretly wonder what happened to the life you dreamt of, and part of you even wonders if it is too late. It's not! You just have to give yourself grace. Grace to release what's no longer working and rebuild the life you want. And that starts today!

I want you to know that what you want is possible.

After six years in business, I closed my concierge service. I established a consulting firm supporting other ambitious women to crush their business goals without sacrificing their sanity, serenity, or self. I run my business with braids in my head and boundaries that allow me to be present for my family and take care of my body.

The many women who have been impacted and have decided that they too will no longer suppress their authentic success live in grace.

- Glaiza accomplished a dream that was ten years in the making by writing her first book, *Waking Up on the Inside*. It also led to her launching a speaking career.

- Anna was frustrated and exhausted in her career and eventually decided it was time to kiss her 9-5 goodbye. She decided to go out on her own, and she pursued her calling of running her consulting firm full-time. My favorite part of her story is that she restored her love and hobby of making jewelry and unexpectedly ended up on the runway during fashion week after a designer saw her work.

- Or Chinere produces one of Baltimore's biggest summers events but wanted to add an arm to her business to curate intentional experiences for couples year-round. She homed in on how to truly start to master her time so that she could scale her business.

As I boarded the plane to head home the evening after the championship game, my knees stiffened a little as I sat in between the narrow seats of the

---

Join our community to see videos of more success stories like these ladies.

plane, and I rubbed them in remembrance of what we had just experienced. As the plane touched down in Maryland, I promised myself there would be no going back to the way things once were.

Burn the boat to anything mediocre. Throw away the doubts and stop second-guessing yourself. Embrace the fear and let it propel you forward, and don't look back. Know that you already have everything you need to succeed. It's time to choose. Choose the path that challenges you, the one that takes you out of your comfort zone, but most importantly, the one you can call your own. Commit to filling your life with moments that make you activate new muscles, access alternative routes, and unlock hidden parts of your personality. And don't forget in the process to **GIVE YOURSELF GRACE, GIRL!**

Rashida McKenzie

$\mathcal{R}$ashida McKenzie trains highly ambitious women to crush their business goals without sacrificing their sanity, serenity, or self. She teaches them to implement systems and build a solid support base. As a speaker, media personality, and coach, Rashida has the privilege of working with women at every level of professional success. She has enjoyed working with women from the White House to founding the first-of-its-kind concierge company helping executive and entrepreneurial moms manage their households all over the Washington, DC area.

As a mom, wife, and businesswoman serving in many roles, Rashida's mission is simple: to provide women with the tools to make their **OWN RULES!**

Check her out at

🌐 www.RashidaMcKenzie.com

📷 www.Instagram.com/RashidaMcK

f www.facebook.com/RashidaMcK

CPSIA information can be obtained
at www.ICGtesting.com
Printed in the USA
BVHW041815050722
641356BV00010B/74